My Sense of Silence

Creative Nonfiction

*A list of books in the series appears
at the end of this book.*

MY SENSE OF *Silence*

Memoirs of a

Childhood with

Deafness

Lennard J. Davis

UNIVERSITY OF ILLINOIS PRESS

URBANA AND CHICAGO

Photo p. 130 by George Zimbel.
Photo p. 145 by Alan L. Marcus.

Library of Congress Cataloging-in-Publication Data
Davis, Lennard J., 1949–
My sense of silence: memoirs of a childhood with deafness /
Lennard J. Davis.
p. cm. — (Creative nonfiction)
Includes bibliographical references.
ISBN 0-252-02533-4 (cloth: alk. paper)
1. Davis, Lennard J., 1949– .
2. Children of deaf parents—United States Biography.
3. Deaf parents—United States Biography.
4. Deaf—United States—Family relationships Case studies.
I. Title.
II. Series.
HQ759.912.D38   2000
306.874'092—dc21   99-6618
[B]   CIP

C 5 4 3 2 1

To Bella,
who suggested that I write down my
family stories

To Carlo and Francesca,
so that my story may be part of theirs

To my brother, Gerald,
who, by reading, understood

And to my CODA brothers and sisters,
whose insights gave me the mind and
heart to understand my childhood

Augustine.—You said you could not imagine being born among such men.

Evodius.—And I say so still; for unless I am mistaken, you admit that the persons to whom you refer were born among speaking people.

Augustine.—I do not deny it; but as we are now agreed that such men do exist, I ask you to consider this question: If a man and a woman of this kind were united in marriage and for any reason transferred to some solitary place, where, however, they might be able to live, if they should have a son who is not deaf, how would the latter speak with his parents?

Evodius.—How can you think that he would do otherwise than reply by gestures to the signs which his parents made to him? However, a small boy could not do even this; therefore my reasoning remains sound. For what does it matter, as he grows up, whether he speaks or makes gestures, since both these pertain to the soul.

—St. Augustine,
   De quantitate animae liber unus

Contents

Preface

I originally intended to write *My Sense of Silence* as a sheer act of memory. I wanted to record my life so that at least some trace of it would be made permanent for my children, Carlo and Francesca. My wife, Bella Mirabella, had long suggested I do so.

This memoir extends to my sophomore year at Columbia during the student strike of 1968. It traces a trajectory from victimization, in a way, to liberation. My parents' deafness and working-class status started out for me as a limitation and have become, through the struggles of Deaf people (perhaps more than of working-class folks in the same period), a mark of distinction and accomplishment.

A few points concerning deafness. First, I generally am not employing the newer usage of "Deaf" indicating Deaf culture—as opposed to "deaf," which refers to the simple fact of hearing impairment. I am invoking a world where that distinction was not made by hearing or Deaf people, although Deaf culture definitely existed. In the world of the 1950s and 1960s the deaf were all too often disempowered and victimized. To use "Deaf" to describe the situation at that time seems anachronistic.

Second, when I have my parents speak, I translate their signs more or less directly into English. As anyone who has used or studied sign language knows, this form of communicating is as fluent and capacious as any language. It is not broken English. My aim is to give readers a sense of the word order of sign language and to create a typographic difference from oral language. As a CODA (Child of Deaf Adults), I exist between sign language and spoken language. My translation is an attempt to render visible the way my mind reads sign language. In fact, CODAs have invented "CODA talk," a verbalized form of sign language.* So: my apologies to anyone who is offended by the way I render sign language, and my counsel to hearing people that the broken quality of the rendering indicates no lack of linguistic ability on my parents' part.

Finally, I made a decision to present my parents to the world as I perceived them, not as they perceived themselves or as other Deaf people perceived them. This is my story, not theirs. Like any child or adolescent, I cannot claim objectivity or even fairness. In *Shall I Say a Kiss?: Courtship Letters of a Deaf Couple* (Gallaudet University Press, 1999), I have edited my parents' correspondence and written about their lives. That volume contains another and more objective portrayal of their characters.

Some Deaf readers and CODAs may be unsettled by parts of this book because it does not only present a glowing picture of being a son of deaf parents. I did not write this book to extol the virtues of the Deaf or of Deaf parents, nor did I write it to question the ability of Deaf people to parent hearing or deaf children. I am proud of my connection with Deafness, but I am only writing about my parents and my particular experience with and of them. I write to recount my memories and feelings, to record the truth as I recall it, to detail the singularities of one life. To have softened or changed what happened might serve some political or public relations end, but it would be false. While one's personal truth may be sometimes unpleasant, it has the virtue of being unassailable.

My thanks to Paul Preston and Jenny Singleton for their advise on the manuscript. Also to Ann Lowry of the University of Illinois Press for shepherding the memoir through the editorial and publication process, and to Pat Hollahan for her aid in copyediting.

---

* See Paul Preston's *Mother Father Deaf* (Cambridge: Harvard University Press, 1996) for a more complex discussion of "CODA talk."

The Grain of Sounds

If one exposes his cattle to the sun, or
he places them in the custody of a deaf-
mute, a fool, or a minor, and they break
away and do damage, he is liable.

—Early Hebrew law

When I lay in bed at night, I did not
experience what most children feel: that sense of security and comfort,
of being in the lap and bosom of the family. Instead, I lay terrified and
cold. I had to listen for every sound, because my parents could not hear
any danger. Even were I to call them from my bed, they could not hear
me. I was alone, small, and helpless.

An early memory, so early I cannot be sure it was in fact my own, is
of hearing my parents making love next to me in the dark. I am an in-
fant. My crib is next to their bed in our one-bedroom apartment, while
my ten-year-old brother, Gerald, is fast asleep in the living room. I hear
groaning, slurping sounds rising out of the blackness, as if the bed were
eating my parents. I cry and scream, twisting in my bedclothes right
next to them, but out of reach. They are making love while I wail in terror—and even though they are inches away from me, they are totally unaware. The barrier of a few feet, insignificant to the hearing, becomes the

widest abyss possible. As my mother's odd voice climaxes, my wails meld into hers.

A child of the deaf may become hypervigilant. This is a word I heard used on the radio to describe soldiers returning from war: they lie in their beds at night, hypervigilant. They wait for the bomb to drop, the shell to explode, the friend to drag his limbless torso into the trench. That was my experience of childhood. I listened for the burglars that my parents could not hear, for the robbers, the monsters, the flash fire, the cracking sounds of a ceiling collapsing. I was the guard, and it was all war.

(Last night I lay in bed listening to the mice running through a farmhouse where I am vacationing. The lights were off; my wife was asleep; I lay in rigid awareness. When I hear sounds in the night, I still panic. My heart pounds. I never wake my wife, and I never woke my parents. I lie, now as then, in silent terror.)

My bedroom overlooked a dark alleyway where the garbage was kept. Every night the feral cats of the South Bronx gathered there, reenacting a feline *West Side Story,* overturning the cans, engaging in spitting fights, and emitting yowls of indescribable horror. One particular sound, perhaps of a male cat in rut or a female in heat, sounded to me like a witch crying. Because my parents were deaf, there was a giant dictionary of sounds for which I had no names. This was one of them. I knew never to ask my brother about the witch sound because he would use the opportunity to terrify me further, adding lurid details about how she ate small children. When I discussed the subject with my friends in the building, they never seemed to have heard the caterwauling.

Because it was nameless, the feline yowl was full of dark dread. I was convinced that it was the shriek of an old lady wandering the streets, a constant reminder of the pain of life and the proximity of death. The sound terrified me, but it also accustomed me to its horror. I thought an actual woman who lived around the corner was the very one who wept and screamed under my window. She had the face of an old crone or a withered pansy, and whenever I saw her I ran away.

I never told my parents of the sound and the fear. How could I explain? They would only say it was nothing—which it was, to them. So I learned early to keep fear to myself. And in the end the screams, the weeping, the snarls, and the hisses became my own.

I was born on September 16, 1949, at Wadsworth Hospital in Washington Heights. My first intersection with language was managed by my father, who typically insisted on his own English-language competence despite his deafness. My father worked as a sewing-machine operator in the garment district, but his passion was race-walking. He decided to name me after an obscure Swedish race-walker whose first name was Lennart. My father changed the "t" to a "d" to Americanize the name, but he retained what he fancied was the Swedish pronunciation. I was called "Lee-nard," a name no one has ever, in my entire life, both pronounced and spelled the way my father intended it. My father decided that my middle name should be Jack, in honor of his uncle. He had never learned that Jack was a nickname.

My parents lived in a one-bedroom walk-up apartment at 1883 Clinton Avenue in the East Tremont Avenue section of the Bronx. Morris and Eva Davis were both completely deaf—"stone deaf," my father used to sign. That puzzled me. Was his ear like a stone? Cold, hard, chiseled, like that of a statue?

By most standards we were poor, but my father, whose motto was "Never say die," thought we were middle class. We did not own a telephone, a car, a record player, or an air conditioner—the consumer products that my friends' parents owned. When I was born we had no television, but my parents bought one shortly after. The story in our family was that Gerald was asked whether he wanted a little brother or a television set. Given this Hobson's choice, the nine-year-old opted for the living object, but when I was born he quickly grew bored with the sleeping, bawling mass of flesh. Soon the television entered the apartment.

We possessed little else. My father was an abstemious man. (When he died in 1981, he had saved over $100,000, no small feat for a factory worker.) The occasional ice cream cone was, to us, a special treasure. We never ate out. We never took long trips.

Perhaps my earliest memory is of being pushed in my baby carriage. A heavy, spring-cushioned carriage, dark blue. The fragrance of warmth and comfort, the sun heating my covers luxuriously. My blankets clutched up around my neck, the shade of the carriage bonnet creating what seemed a small, safe world inside. My eyes are fixed on my mother's torso bobbing up and down as she pushes me along. Her face is hidden by the bonnet of the carriage. The yellow five-story apartment buildings of the Bronx and an occasional tree move along the periphery of my vision.

A few years ago I realized that this memory was in fact not pleasant but nightmarish. I had blocked out the negative feelings, like a person who tries to convince himself that an injection will not hurt. One night I was flying in a particularly bad storm. As the plane lurched, I began to feel trapped and helpless. Suddenly the baby carriage appeared to me. No longer was I warm and comfortably cooing; instead, I was screaming, bound in my blankets, twisting and caught, as my mother's torso implacably rose and fell. I could see her, but she could not see my face or hear my cries.

A second memory is of myself walking, no longer bound to the carriage. I leave my mother in the kitchen and wander into the bathroom. There the window above the toilet beckons to me. I climb onto the toilet and then pull myself up to the narrow ledge of the window sill. I survey the bathroom from this dizzying height and grow terrified. The tiles of the floor loom like so many hard slabs waiting to receive the gift of my crumpled body. I cannot move. I scream one long call for my mother. Silence. Another call. More silence. After what seems like a day of screams, my mother appears. She lifts me down off the window ledge as I cry. "I came because I wondered why you so quiet," she says, my screams only silence to her. I can still feel the terror of that abandonment. I have always been susceptible to movies in which heroes hang over tremendous cliffs, with villains stomping on their knuckles, or in which actors traverse high parapets and narrow walkways far above the city traffic.

A further memory of separation. In a closet between the living room and the bedroom my parents keep a whip as a threat to my brother and me. I sneak into the closet to explore, closing the door to keep out unwanted eyes. But there is no doorknob on the inside, only a stump of metal. I am trapped in utter darkness, with things draped on me like pendant moss from the wild woods or the suspicion of fingers in the night. I call to my mother. Then I scream but nothing happens. I hear her feet walk within inches of me as I pound on the closet door. I can't remember if I finally opened the door by twisting the small remnant of the knob, or whether my mother decided to look in. To me this is an essential but unanswerable question: Did help come from within, or from without?

I also locked myself in the bathroom. Normally we never latched the bathroom or any other door, but on this occasion a girl had come over to play with me and my alphabet blocks, and when I went to the bathroom, in a moment of prudishness, I locked the door. When I tried to unlock the door, I was not strong enough to turn the lock handle. My playmate heard me crying and directed my mother to the bathroom. My mother tried to instruct me through the door, but she could not hear my questions. I struggled with the handle, crying, and finally the door opened.

One day I went with my mother to the Crotona Park swimming pool. My brother and his friends used to call it "The Inkwell" because it was mainly patronized by African Americans. I was too young to understand racism and to go along with its attendant crass humor, and too young to swim, so I spent much of my time looking into the water to see if it really was dark as ink. My mother was asleep tanning on a lounge chair, so I went to the toilet alone. On the way back I stopped to look into the depths. As I was staring below the churning waters and writhing bodies, actually beginning to think I could see dark hues, a boy came up behind me and pushed me in. I remember the moment clearly: suspended under water, one arm rising languidly above my head, watching with a strange detachment as breath escapes in ellipses from my mouth like comic-book thoughts and rises through the silent water. A calm, blue-green, peaceful feeling enveloped me as I watched my life slip away in the bubbles. I knew I was going to die in the beautiful, silent water. How would anyone ever see me under the violent froth of noisy, screaming children? The water imposed an abrupt deafness on my world, a deafness that felt familiar and right.

Suddenly a hand grasped my hand, the one floating above my head, and pulled me from the blue silence into the noisy, fractious air. I was born again, this time like Venus in the Bronx. I burst into tears then and ran to find my mother. I can't remember what she said; perhaps she cautioned me to be more careful. I realized then more clearly than ever that my screams could not be heard, that in this noisy world I must rely on my own wits and hands, and on the kindness of strangers. I always regretted that I never thanked the owner of that hand for pulling me out.

My first "word" was "milk." I said it in sign language, reaching my little hands out from the crib. The sign for "milk" in my family was two closed fists rubbing knuckles together up and down in a loose imitation of milking a cow.* I was six months old, according to my parents. That I signed before I spoke proves what scientists now have discovered: children of the deaf babble with their fingers, just as children of the hearing babble with their tongues.

Sign was my native language. It is a language inextricably tied to my inner feelings, more so than speech. To a native signer who can also hear, there is a strong and nostalgic feeling about sign language that is inextricably connected to earliest childhood. To this day if I sign "milk," I feel more milky than if I say the word. When I make the sign and facial gestures for "hate"—a face contorted with anger as both hands hurl the hate with flinging fingers—I feel the kind of hate a child feels, emotion

---

* My parents' sign language was a mixture of British Sign Language and American Sign Language. Many of our "home signs" were therefore anomalous when compared with current U.S. usage.

unmediated by polite adult expectations. Likewise "love," indicated by crossing arms against chest and giving oneself a hug, feels far more encompassing and visceral than the word "love" stated with the lips.

My feelings toward sign language are now tinged by the fact that, for me, it is somewhat of a lost language. My parents are both dead, and I have few people with whom I can sign. I feel like the expatriate wandering the boulevards of Paris but hearing with the inner ear the lost language of home, the music of the Russian steppes or the Polish countryside. Although sign is actively spoken among the Deaf, my contacts with Deaf people have only recently been reestablished. I am no longer part of that community, but part of me wants to go home to it.

Hearing people who see sign language may think of it as a substitute language inferior to speech. Research by Deaf and hearing linguists has proven that sign language is neither a substitute for English nor impoverished speech. The abbé de l'Epée, an eighteenth-century priest, is generally regarded as the "father" of sign language. He did not invent it; rather, as the story goes, he stumbled upon two deaf girls in the countryside talking to each other. His mission, as he saw it, was to codify and render "grammatical" the natural language of the urban deaf of Paris. He and others attempted to make the grammar of sign language look like that of French or English. But languages do not need grammarians to rectify them; they are self-contained systems. Wherever deaf people are thrown together, sign language will arise. The deep structure of the human brain contains language that will come out, whatever the medium. For people who are prelingually deaf, it is difficult to acquire spoken language. Language, like water, will find the path of least resistance, and words flow through their fingers.

American Sign Language was a variant of the French version, imported by Thomas Gallaudet, an American who visited the abbé's institute and brought back a deaf teacher, Laurent Clerc, to Hartford, where the first U.S. school for the deaf was founded. American Sign Language does not resemble English, and in many cases its verb structure is richer and more complex than that of English. Grammatically and structurally,

ASL displays different uses of tense, case, word order, and morphemes than English. As a child I did not know this, nor did my parents. In fact, we did not really think sign was a legitimate language; we were taught that it was a kind of pidgin, a systematized use of gesture. So I simply tended to enjoy the physical nature of sign language, its sheer muscular energy and pictorial poetics, although I felt it was inferior to speech.

Since the mid-nineteenth century, hearing teachers of the deaf have had a strong aversion toward the use of sign language in schooling. Earlier, when all teachers of the deaf were deaf themselves, they taught in sign. But at the now infamous Milan Conference of 1880, sign language was banned from educational institutions throughout the world. After that, the hearing taught the deaf.* I remember my mother's stories of having to sign in secret at her residential school in England, avoiding the patrolling eyes of her teachers.

Signing is like speech set to dance. There is a constant pas de deux between the fingers and the face. Since the features must express tone and volume, the face is continually mirroring the meaning of the fingers. There are combinations of small-motor skills, quick finger darts, and large sweeps with the arms and the body. Those who do not know sign language can only see the movements as distant and unnuanced. But those who understand signing can see the finest shade of meaning in a gesture. Like the pleasure some hearing people take in the graded distinctions between words like "dry," "arid," "parched," "desiccated," or "dehydrated," so the deaf can enjoy equivalent distinctions in the gestures of sign language. Appreciating these is like appreciating the differences between certain sopranos singing famous arias or the subtle flavors in food. Even to this day, as I walk along the street and observe hearing people, I see them speaking a sort of language with their hands. Like monkeys at typewriters or like raving schizophrenics, they are making occasional sense in random ways.

---

* See Douglas Baynton's *Forbidden Signs: American Culture and the Campaign against Sign Language* (Chicago: University of Chicago Press, 1996) for more information on this subject.

I recently came to a series of uncanny revelations about sign language. For years I thought I knew sign language, although I never really used it except at home. After my parents died, I never used it at all, except when I might want to recall some special childhood feeling or simply talk to myself in an intimate and private way. When I became involved with CODA and saw other hearing people signing, I found it hard to understand much of what they were saying, and I was reluctant to converse in sign language. Then I began to be convinced that I could not speak sign language at all. Some experts told me that what I was speaking at home was really "home-sign," a combination of sign language, speech, gesture, and whatever worked to get my parents to understand me. Did that mean my communication with my parents was always faulty? Had I actually created my own language, instead of receiving one that had been worked out for me by millions of signers long dead? (Another example of having to take care of myself?) Perhaps the seeds of thought that germinated in my mind lacked good earth to grow in. Instead, they welled up inside me. I could ask for a hug, food, daylight; but I could not say what needed to be said, except imperfectly. No wonder writing has held me in such a thrall.

This insight seemed true for two years. Then, at my third CODA convention, I had a breakthrough. One day I was watching the blur of sign language, and the next day I could understand everything. Was it just that familiarity had revived my memory, or had I refused to *let* myself understand? Had I cut myself off from deafness, from my parents, and until this moment failed to forge the chains that would reconnect me?

Shortly after, one day when I was on a long drive alone, I began to sign to myself. (This form of talking to oneself must be practiced a bit if one wants to stay on the road.) I realized I was talking to my father. He had always corrected my signing with a little "x" in the air that meant "correction." Or he would make the sign for "wrong," a fist with finger and thumb extended crashing against the chin, with an exasperated sneer. As I swerved down the highway, I was signing furiously to him in my mind: "You made me feel that I couldn't speak sign language. You wanted it for yourself. But sign language is *mine*. It was my first language. I spoke it in the cradle. It is mine as well as yours. And I want it back!" It may be true that my parents had wanted me to speak English and so had discouraged my use of sign language. But now I felt determined to make sign language my own, and to make words flow from my hand like flowers growing from the earth.

Even though they never heard my voice, the sounds of my parents' voices are still in my ears. To most people, the deaf sound strange, guttural and strangulated. To me, the normal voices of the deaf are soothing, like whale sounds, cooing and arcing under the surface of the deep. I hear sounds effortless and liquid, too high pitched for human voices, too low for birds. The consonants are not generally sharp enough, the vowels too open. The rising and falling tones of English are strangely absent, replaced by rising and falling that come from the logic of breath and the length of words. This is a pure poetry of sound.

Not all deaf speak alike. The first aural distinction I made was between my parents' voices. Father's voice was gruff, guttural and unclear, as if it emerged from the bottom of a deep well. He tried to speak very clearly for hearing people, slowly articulating each word as best as he could. But it was like trying to mold molasses. No matter how sharply he formed his words, they always came out muddy and rough. He thought he spoke quite well—better than my mother, and he prided himself on the medals he had received for lip-reading while at residential school. But by hearing standards he spoke unclearly. Most people had trouble understanding him as he painstakingly repeated his phrases. He would get angry at people who missed his meaning, and he would repeat after each phrase "Un-der-stand-me?" as if he were speaking to somewhat slow children. If he had to resort to writing a phrase, he would shake his head at the dullness of the hearing person.

Once, when I was a child, he nearly got into a fight with a teenage gang member in our apartment building. My father saw him light a match to peer into the bank of mailboxes in the narrow entryway. My father tried to tell him not to do that because he might set the letters on fire. Comprehending only the gruff reproof, the young man shoved my father. They almost came to blows. The incident was not atypical of my father's interactions with the hearing world: he liked to tell people what they were doing wrong, and often he was perceived as belligerent.

The sign for a hearing person is made by putting the forefinger under the lower lip and moving it out in small circles, as if words were coming out. A deaf person indicates deafness by pointing with the forefinger to the ear and then bringing the finger perpendicular to the lips. It is about that strange thing that hearing people do, moving their mouths open and closed all the time. Accounts of deaf children in deaf families discovering the hearing world always express a kind of mystification about what others are doing with their mouths. They just keep moving them and refuse to sign. Speaking is hearing.

My father rightly hated being called "deaf and dumb." His lifelong cause was to convince hearing people that he was not "dumb." Dumb did not mean mute to my father; it meant stupid. He did not want to be called stupid by the hearing world (although he called *me* "stupid" all the time). But my father never really could accept the difficulty hearing people had with his speech. He felt that if he was articulating, then he was communicating. Given the discrimination against deaf people, it probably never occurred to him (or to others) that hearing people were limited by their never having learned sign language.

As he prided himself on his speech, he prided himself on his sign language. He thought of himself as the Cicero of the New York deaf world. I never thought much about his technique, focusing instead on his content. After he died, I was surprised to learn from his Deaf friend that some deaf had found him not such a smooth signer; his signs were not crisp and clear, or lilting and poetic, in the various ways that the deaf admire signing.

When he died, I did learn from many of the mourners at his funeral that he was highly regarded as a parliamentarian among the deaf. He knew *Robert's Rules of Order* by heart. No surprise there, since he lived by rules and mottoes: "Cross bridge when come to it." "Willful waste makes woeful want." "When eat must have potatoes." "Bad read in bed." "Bad read on toilet." "Never say die." "Always wash hands." "Never wear pajamas out of bed." The commandments rolled down to my little ears like silent thunder from Zion. Some he had learned at school, some he read, and some he just invented.

My mother's voice, by contrast, was high and liquid. It had the quality that a coin has as it spins on a glass table top. It almost squealed, yet beneath was a silver hum. Her voice was like bird song floating down almost without substance. It always surprised by its strangeness of tone.

My mother, Eva Weintrobe, was born in Liverpool in 1911. She had a large, close family with two sisters and two brothers. Her father was a thin, wiry cabinetmaker with sad, sloping eyes; her mother was a small, thin woman whose features were all slits in the sunlight. At seven, my mother contracted spinal meningitis—what they called "brain fever." She was taken to hospital, where they shaved her head and soaked her in ice water. The fever lasted for weeks. She appeared to be dying. She remembers awaking from her delirium and looking at her mother's face. She saw that her mother was talking to her, but she could not hear the sound. Characteristically, she told me this without emotion. Her favorite motto was "Don't cry over spilled milk."

One day from the balcony of the hospital she saw her friends walking to school, talking and laughing. She saw them but couldn't hear them. She then realized fully the surroundings of silence. But she hid from them because she did not want them to laugh at her shaved head. Such a telling thing about childhood: Was it her shaved head, rather than her deafness, that embarrassed her? Probably both.

My mother's voice was frozen in the lower-class accent of Jewish Liverpool in 1918. Apparently linguists are always looking for such people so they can study those accents from times before there were tape recorders. When new sounds are shut off from people, their extant phonemes become somewhat distorted over time. My mother's voice always seemed muffled and distant, from far over the sea and long ago. I can hear her calling me from the window of our tenement. A long, high-pitched strand of sound pitched out into the yellow air of the Bronx summer. Her call always reached my ears, but my reply never reached hers—a one-way umbilicus. Her voice was always out of place as it punctured my stick-ball game; embarrassing and alien, but alluring. I always came.

My mother's pronunciation was far better than my father's, since she was not prelingually deaf, but we all colluded and enabled my father to feel that his speech was superior. (When "Don't cry over spilled milk" meets "Never say die," there really is no match.) My mother deferred to my father on most issues, letting him handle business transactions and other official dealings with the outside world. But my mother always had hearing friends, whereas my father really did not, except in the realm of sports.

Both of my parents were identified with what we now call "Deaf culture," but both were proud that they could mix with hearing people. Some CODAs believe the hearing world is the enemy, the place of the other. My parents did not feel that way. They groomed me and my brother to be their substitutes in that world, the way that Miss Havisham groomed Estella in *Great Expectations*. I am not sure we were supposed to break hearts, but we were supposed to succeed, to overcome barriers that they, in their era, could not.

I don't remember when I realized that I could hear and that my parents were deaf. I probably always knew. I recall no shock of realization, just succeeding moments that had to be swallowed so life could carry on. ("Don't cry over spilled milk." "Never say die.") But it became clear that hearing was my talent, my destiny. Unlike many CODAs, my brother and I had no name signs. A name sign is literally a special sign, rather like a nickname, given to each person. In the Deaf community, people usually get name signs at school, often for some distinguishing physical trait. My mother's name sign was made by holding the flattened hand, fingers toward the face, and pushing the extended fingers just below the mouth. This evoked her buck teeth. My father's sign was made by taking the index finger and sliding over the cleft in the chin to emphasize that it was rather indented. But my brother and I were always called by our hearing names. The point was clear: we were not to be culturally Deaf.

Although I considered myself culturally Deaf, my parents did not. Like the light-skinned African American in a family who might hope to deny racial markers, my parents wanted me to pass. Passing would mean not showing any aspect of deaf culture in my body language, facial gestures, or communication. I complied. My teachers and relatives were all impressed with how "normal" I was, how "well" I communicated. I did not grunt and mime like my father, but I lived two lives. Like many bilingual people, I could code-switch easily. Recently, visiting Gallaudet University for the first time, I was struck by how a hearing student of mine who had gone on to become a professor at that institution had developed his signing to include these sounds and gestures. He wanted to imitate the way Deaf people sign. I became even more aware of how I edited them out.

It was actually my wife who first called my attention to the fact that, only when I spoke with my father, my entire face changed. It became "deaf." Even my voice changed to accompany my exaggerated mouthings of the words that went along with my signs. I spoke with a British accent, the lost Liverpudlian accent from 1918 that my mother had brought to America with her. I possessed two modes of communicating, and I had built an inviolable firewall between them.

Now, since I have been dealing with these issues more openly, I find that I am just growing able to show my "deaf" face and voice to hearing people. When I do readings about Deafness or disability, I make it a point to sign, to use my face in Deaf ways, and to let this imprisoned child out of his cell—to let him speak like Kaspar Hauser being let out of his prison. The feeling is liberating. I can be Deaf for the first time.

Silence has always haunted me. I fear it, yet I seek it. In silence I lose my boundaries. I expand to fill the room, the forest, the sky. This loss of self terrifies me. The only way I knew to exist against the silence was to make noise. Whimpers, sniffs, throat-clearings, song—these sounds let me know I was there. I still burst into song, and talk to myself, and of course I write. If others couldn't hear me, at least I could hear myself. Writing confirms me against silence. When I write, I am knocking from inside the coffin.

What is silence? The absence of sound. Yet one can hear it. It sounds like something. It has a hum, a pitch. What are we hearing?

In silence now as I write, I am sitting at a long, black desk in a Tuscan farmhouse. The room is large and whitewashed with red-brick floors. The sunlight forms a bright square on the brick, and the rest of the room recedes into a chiaroscuro darkness. I look out onto a row of grapevines warming in the sun. The birds set up a constant Italian argument, and the insects join the drone. It is a moment of apparent silence, yet not silent enough. Chickens cluck, a child murmurs, the wind rustles through the cypress trees.

Only the kind of deafness my parents had brings total silence—lack of sound so vivid that there is no pulse of blood rushing through the ears. A silence that flattens vision, that makes the living landscape a portrait on a damp wall where foreground and background become one. A sensual experience in which the eye, the hand, the nose, and the taste buds rule.

My visual sense has always been acute. I need to combine sight and sound. When I go to a concert, I must see the violinist, view the strings of the cello. When I look at the world, I expect it to speak to me. My parents looked at the world, and it remained silent. When they were in a room, they were never elsewhere. They could not be in one place but hear another. Everything was here and now. Sound takes you outside yourself, around corners, behind doors. If my aim is to be in my moment, I have failed dismally. I am always around the corner, beyond myself, checking the distance, being aware—hypervigilant.

2

Language and the Word of My Father

Tell X that speech is not dirty silence
Clarified. It is silence made still dirtier
—Wallace Stevens, "The Creation of
   Sounds"

Coming into spoken language was all too easy for me. That world, at least, was all mine. Most children live in an imaginative space where they can say or do anything. I had that space in the daily world, at least in terms of language. Face to face, I belonged to my parents' world and the world of sign language. But with the face averted, the world was my own. The public world of speech was my private idiom.

Facing toward me, my father could be imposing, frightening. Facing away from me, he was inconsequential, the butt of many of my and my brother's jokes. Unlike God in the Garden of Eden, our father did not know what he could not see. When his face was turned from us, we had our paradise, our playground where we might frolic without fear. Of course, there was always the possibility that his face would turn back. He would ask us what we were laughing about. Him, often; but we would lie and say it was just a joke one of us had told. He had to accept that excuse, although it did not satisfy him.

We, on the other hand, could always be duplicitous. We made comments through our smiling lips and gritted teeth. We would say he was a dumb fool, a Russian spy, and other rude things in front of him. If he could not see our lips move, then we were silent. My aim was to make my noise his silence.

My father's face was handsome. Relatives and friends told me he was handsome, and my mother agreed. Fifty-two when I was born, he appeared youthful, despite his baldness. A pencil-thin moustache made him look like the movie idols of the twenties and thirties: Leslie Howard, with a bit of Clark Gable.

Though they said he was handsome, from my small perspective he often looked grotesque. His nose reminded me of Jimmy Durante; his baldness did too, and also of Eisenhower. His baggy trousers were the style in the fifties, but they made him seem comical, like Charlie Chaplin. I associated flatulence and bad odors with the folds of those pants. Being deaf, he shared the occupational hazard of not being able to hear his own farts. The auditory offense did not exist except as manifest in an olfactory phenomenon. He would blithely pass his gas, and at my level I was a direct recipient of something whose existence I could not assert. However, when it came to detecting the anal transgressions of others, my father blamed me. If he smelled any waft of sulfur, his solution was to turn to me and tell me sternly to go to the bathroom. I became the whipping boy for the farts of others. In fact, I was blamed for anything that went awry in the family, since I was the youngest and hence the most likely to cause disruption.

I have a powerful memory of a man who was wearing a pair of baggy pants like my father's. He was standing in front of me and my mother as we waited under the Third Avenue El for the Short Line bus to the Catskills, en route to visit my Uncle Joe, the rabbi of the Concord Hotel. The seat of the man's trousers was directly at my eye level. There in front of me, inches away, was a squashed caterpillar, still vaguely wiggling. The man had obviously sat on this caterpillar and was now inadvertently displaying its ghastly remains to a four-year-old. As the line moved forward toward the bus, my mother kept pushing me into the man's pants and into the caterpillar's oozing innards. I remember staring at the caterpillar with disgust. Was it disgust about my father? A reminder of myself, so small, squashed up against my father's giant being? Was it disgust for my mother's useless pushing? Or for my own silence? In writing this memoir, I feel I must include the caterpillar; I am sure of its importance, but I may never know its significance.

As a child I often feared my father more than I loved him. He was a brusque man whose anxiety could explode. While I realize now that he had a lot to be anxious about, he always refused to think of himself as nervous. He would insist that he was perennially calm, even though his hands always vibrated with a fine tremor.

Despite his mood swings, from brooding dejection to anxiety, he and I did have playful times together. My favorite moments with him were on Sunday mornings. My parents would be asleep on the high-riser bed in the living room—a single mattress on a metal frame from which another single bed would roll out and then, with a deft pull, rise up to meet its match. Since my brother was nearly ten years older, he was roiled in adolescent sleep-death for most mornings of my early childhood. I would wander through the apartment, looking for fun in what often seemed a mortuary.

I developed a game that involved crawling into the spring mechanism under the high-riser bed while my parents slept. I would wedge myself into some ridiculously small cul-de-sac of metal and springs and pretend I was crawling through the inner workings of a submarine. I was reenacting a scene that was generic to visual narratives of the era in which a sailor, sweating profusely, crawls into the claustrophobia-inducing torpedo bay and defuses an about-to-explode missile as the other sweating members of the crew watch the ticking clock. My favorite television show was "The Silent Service," a program that opened with an overhead shot of a submarine cleaving the ocean and emerging to the accompaniment of triumphant music. Somehow the silence and the ocean triggered images of deafness, claustrophobia, and symbolic birth canals. I would then bounce my small body off various pieces of metal and ricochet along the dusty floor, imagining I was passing through narrow tunnels beneath the silent depths.

It was only a matter of time before my father or mother awoke after some particularly active propulsion. My father was usually the first to wake, and I would crawl into bed with him. My mother's bed was the section of the high-riser that went under my father's, in a sort of permanent tribute to the missionary position. Because the two beds were separated by a small divide, my father and I could have a wrestling tickle fight without disturbing her. I loved those moments of physical closeness with my father. Since he was really much like a child emotionally, and I often not a child at all, it was one of the few situations where we could actually make contact with each other on a physical level.

But the bad times with him were more common. Then his face would become to me a terrifying mask of anger or contempt. The faces of deaf people are used in sign language much more than those who use speech and so serve as better canvases on which to paint emotion. The face must carry the message of *tone* in conversation. In speaking aloud, one can indicate how firm a "no" is by modulating the voice. One can utter "no" in a way that indicates "perhaps," or even "yes." But a deaf person's face must carry this inflection. Such mobility can be especially disconcerting to a child, for whom the face of the father is so large, so imposing.

Too often my father's face reflected disappointment, disgust, or anxiety—emotions that flowed like a brackish stream beneath the surface of his gaze. At other times his face could be illuminated with childish pleasure writ large.

My earliest specific memory of a paternal face is a terrifying one, yet it is not actually that of my father. I recall being in my baby carriage crying, and a man with a brimmed hat and a pencil-thin moustache peered in and hissed "Shhhh!" Perhaps a great many men in the Bronx wore brimmed hats and sported pencil-thin mustaches around 1950? My terror came from the fact that the man looked like my father—but was not. This moment of *unheimlich,* of the "uncanny" as Freud described it, is the most terrifying because something familiar is turned into something unfamiliar while still retaining aspects of its familiarity. The face of the man in the brimmed hat darkened the opening of my baby carriage, intruded into my space and filled me with terror. My father would never have said "Shhhh!" because he could not hear me; I think I also must have intuited that he would have had to look at me first to see that I was crying. This "what's-wrong-with-this-picture" scenario simply provoked my panic and fear.

Where was my mother? Probably buying fruit at the fruit stand. Perhaps the man only intended to calm a crying child whose mother was unaware of his tears. But I received this message: "Be silent or I will kill you." The rule of silence that goes with forms of exile, and always with cunning, was laid down by that *unheimlich* father. I learned early that tears are to be kept to oneself. What is admired is self-control, the appearance of strength. Silence and discretion.

Oppressed by some in the hearing world, my father often took out his anger on us. I see his face most clearly telling me, in contorted, fully realized rage, that I am filthy and stupid. "Filthy" expressed with the back of the four fingers of the right hand wiggling under the chin (also the sign for "pig"). "Stupid" expressed by taking the clenched fist and rapping knuckles on the brow. I cannot remember what I was filthy and stupid about, but to fulfill his judgment, I succeed in being as filthy and stupid as possible. My filthy acts include picking my nose and putting my snot on the night table next to my bed, not washing my hands whenever possible, reading on the toilet. This latter injunction—never read on the toilet—was strictly enforced by my father, although I could not figure out what was filthy about this, except for a general miscegenation of books and feces. I rebelled by studiously reading the advertising copy on the Fab detergent box under the bathroom sink. But my supreme act of rebellion—an early expression of rage and delight—involved the TV.

The television set was as close as we came to having a sacred object in our house. To me, the roundish screen of the Emerson console was simply my father's face in another guise. "The Emerson console" is a phrase that neither my brother nor I can utter even now without a quaver of reverence. The set was a substitute pleasure object in my family after the brief thrill of having a new child was over and the disappointment of added responsibility set in.

The Emerson console focused all my father's anxieties. The television brought the hearing world into the house, but my father could not hear it. If he could not control the hearing world, at least he could control the TV. There were more rules associated with the television set than with any other object we owned, and our house was rule driven. I was not allowed to touch the TV at all. Since it was the most expensive thing we owned, we all had to pay dearly. Once the TV was there, my father worshiped it. Like all gods, it alternately rewarded and punished him. The television set was often broken, either off at the repair shop or just recently repaired. Because my father clung to a belief in an orderly world, when the television began its decline, he knew that there was a reason. He obviously could not be the cause of the television's wrath; he was, after all, an observant worshiper. Since everyone else in the family was older than I was, whenever the television broke it had to be my fault. Here was a logic to shame that of Socrates.

The rules associated with the TV were vast, varied, and inviolable. First, one could not switch channels without removing one's hand completely from the knob for each click. Switching from channel 2, for example, to channel 11 involved a complex, almost balletic set of gestures. A pronounced flourish accompanied each removal of the hand from the knob to illustrate to the ever-watching father—or just to show the television itself—that rules were being observed. Wrenching of the knob was a punishable crime. Wrenching was a vice practiced by *others*.

Others were on my father's mind a good deal: they lived outside our house and did everything wrong. Even though most *others* were hearing, they were forever twisting the knobs on their televisions—this, to the eternal delight of Ruby around the corner. Ruby made what seemed enormous amounts of money fixing the Emerson console. My father was convinced that these repairs were trumped up, clearly the product of Ruby's greed rather than the result of any abuse in our house. Unlike the *others,* we did everything right—as long as we did what father said we should do. There was always the clear and present danger that my brother and I would slide over into becoming *others*—co-conspirators with Ruby. Actually, we knew all along that we already were. And so was my father, since it was clear that only *others* could cause television sets to break. If our television set broke, then *others* had to be in our house. The logic was overwhelming.

Once the television set had been turned off, it could not be turned on again for ten minutes. This rule had something to do with vacuum tubes and surging currents. The television had to be preserved from wrenching and jolting. Like a hermit or a saint, it had to be spared the thousand natural shocks of the noisy world. This rule somehow combined in my mind with the Jewish dietary laws that said one could not eat dairy products for three hours after one had eaten meat. The waiting period for eating, and for television, seemed logical and even good.

At the center of the television was the Holiest of Holies. The little golden metal cover emblazoned with the Emerson logo covered the control knobs—actually more like small metal posts—labeled "horizontal," "vertical," "contrast," and "brightness." I was not sure what this meant. These knobs were so sacrosanct that only the high priest of the family, my father, was allowed to open the cover.

I began by secretly opening it and gazing upon the horizontal and vertical controls. The pleasure of the forbidden gaze cannot be described. Amazingly enough, I was not struck dead immediately. After realizing that my father's omnipotence was actually a limited power, I began opening the cover whenever he was not around. I was even emboldened to twist the knob ever so slightly one way or another. I don't think I connected my furtive actions with the painstaking hours of adjustment that ensued in the evening, when my father had to twist and turn the knobs in order to watch his ball games.

My father was always suspicious of us. Particularly he feared that we might watch television during the daytime when he was not around. (Another rule: no television until after supper.) Before he left for work each day, he would memorize the position of the channel selector and the rabbit-ear antenna, also noting the pattern of dust atop the console. He would later return home and announce to me that I had used the television. I would, of course, deny the accusation, even if it was true. But I felt a deep reverence for his omniscience, until I discovered the rational explanation for his knowledge and learned to take countermeasures of my own.

My ultimate triumph over the parental injunction was achieved when I began peeing behind the television set. My initial action was motivated by fear: I was afraid to go all the way to the bathroom at night. My father's abstemiousness included a darkened living room. (After all, why waste electricity? "Willful waste makes woeful want.") I had to traverse the living room to reach the bathroom, and my brother spent a good deal of time prepping me for an encounter with the bogeyman who resided there. He explained that the bogeyman was mean, ate children like myself, and only came out in the dark. So I would set out, with full bladder and trepidation, across the darkened living room. I just about made it to where the television stood. Since there was a small space between the armchair and the console, I managed to relieve myself there.

I now question my memory of this causality, because sometimes I would also pee behind the television during the day. If I was afraid of the bogeyman, why would I choose to pee in his very lair? In any case, my memory is of peeing in the silence, in the heart of the darkness. No one could see. No one could hear.

Things went pretty well until one night when the God of Television finally displayed wrath and anger. As I began my usual practice, there were blue flames and smoke, a dank electrical smell, and a loud hiss like thousands of electrified snakes. The solution I had been delivering for days had finally created a major short circuit. I ran in terror to the brightly lit kitchen, where my father read the *Daily News,* my mother washed the dishes, and my brother listened to the radio. I told no one.

Later I was discovered by certain telltale odors and moisture, and I was brought to trial and convicted of first-degree stupidity and filth. I could never tell anyone anything. My parents would dismiss me, and my brother would betray me. In that intersection, between dismissal and disaster, I grew up.

One of the few instances when my father actually spanked me occurred under the watchful gaze of the television. The Brooklyn Dodgers seemed poised to lose a World Series game, much to my father's dismay. He was a devoted Dodgers fan, even though we lived in the Bronx and should have rooted for the Yankees, as I halfheartedly did. (I liked their name better: dodging sounded unheroic to me.) Although he was a maniacal fan, my father never once attended a baseball game. It was too much expense and trouble. He could see and understand what was going on better on television than out in the hearing world. He liked sitting in his own living room, where the greatest danger was misplaced urine streams.

He would move a vinyl-covered chair from the kitchen table into the dead center of the room so that he was directly in line with the television set. It was somehow characteristic of my family that the TV was placed in the living room facing no visible seating—more for wall coverage than for convenience. Either one moved a few chairs in from the kitchen, or else one sat on the couch and performed contortions to catch a glimpse of the video image.

On this particular day, with the Dodgers in the final throes of losing the Series, for some reason even I was present, sensing the defeat about to crash down on the Dodgers and, by extension, on us. They hadn't dodged well enough. My father was a tense knot of muscles and tendons perched on the vinyl chair. He was twitching and muttering and clearing his throat. As the last pitch was thrown, hit, and caught, my father looked glum and signed "Lost." At that moment I, who had never cared a bit about baseball beyond the funniness of Pee Wee Reiss's name and the promise of the young Mickey Mantle, walked up to the black-and-white face of the television and pretended to kick the screen. I say "pretended" because the ensuing events turn on the significance of that intention.

My father saw me approach the sacred Emerson and then, to his horror, beheld my foot almost smashing the screen. I thought I was expressing solidarity with my father's fanatical love of baseball. I would show everyone that I felt disappointed and angry with the Dodgers or with their opponents, even as my cartoon shows were being preempted by extra innings. By my pretend kick I would create a visual equivalent of solidarity with my father. But all he saw was the foot and the screen. I couldn't explain that I was only *pretending* to kick, and in a moment he was yelling in his loud, guttural voice and chasing me around the living room. Obviously he was focusing his own disappointment at the defeat on the small boy with the daring foot. I had never before tried to run away from my father. What followed was a ludicrous chase around the coffee table, a Keystone Kops moment that filled me with terror and made it impossible for me to stop.

The chase ended with my father grabbing me, pulling my pants down, and spanking me on the vinyl chair. I can't recall him ever spanking me before that. My brother, who had been spanked many times before, had forewarned me that if you were spanked and did not cry, you would never be spanked again. Unsure whether this was actual family policy or simply my brother's inventions, I was determined to pass the test. I held my tears in for that spanking, which was the first and last. But it took me thirty years to learn how to release that cry.

While he sat on that vinyl kitchen chair, watching the ball game on TV, he kept the sound off. Perhaps he thought the set might use less electricity? Or that the audio mechanism might avoid inevitable demise and the ensuing repair at Ruby's fix-it shop? By watching the umpire's hand signals, he could follow the game and meet the hearing world on its own gestural terms. Since my father was British, he initially knew nothing about baseball; my brother taught him the rules of the game. But once my father learned, he took off like a fledgling from the nest. My brother used to say he had created Frankenstein's monster. The term seemed appropriate for my father, who, with his rough, inarticulate voice and moody temper swings, reminded us of Boris Karloff in his greatest role.

As the pitcher wound up, Dad would tense in his chair. As the ball sped toward the batter, he would react physically, as if he were swinging at it. His body would rotate slightly, shifting and creaking against the vinyl. Abstracted sucking sounds always accompanied his tension. If the batter connected for a hit, my father would leap up in his excitement, his verbal ejaculations keyed to the number of bases achieved. The crowning moment would, of course, be the home run—preferably driven out of the park. Then he would leap up and yell in his full gutturality, "Home Run. Home Run. Lee-nard. Come. Home Run." Although it was my duty to come into the living room to view this supreme achievement, by the time I got up from playing with my cavalry soldiers, no runners remained on the field, every one having cleared the bases. I was doomed to be late, like the wedding guest in *The Ancient Mariner.*

And I was doomed to listen to my father's frenzied account of who hit what over which wall. I rarely understood these explanations. To me, things were fairly simple. The Dodgers were the ones with the masks— the umpire and the catcher—because they were obviously the ones who dodged. All the rest were the Yankees. The game consisted of watching the Yankees throw the ball at the Dodgers. I preferred the peace and tranquility of the cavalry eternally crouching with their guns or riding nobly on their steeds. Leave the dodging and the yanking to men named Pee Wee or Yogi or Mickey. Still, I had to pause to see the glint in my father's eye as the ordinary moment turned into the transcendent. At those times I saw my father truly joyful. He loved baseball, the sport he could understand, and he could identify with the triumph of winning against the odds.

The God of Television had many tricks. The most terrifying one hovered over Gabby Hayes. Gabby was an old man with a grizzled beard—sort of the chuck-wagon cook type. Given today's television standards it seems unimaginable that such a grizzled old man could host a show. I felt the incongruousness of this old coot being on television, and I was always terrified of him. At the end of his show, Gabby would wheel out a giant cannon that he filled with rice or oats, and then he pointed the cannon directly at the viewing audience and shot the whole farinaceous mess—point blank! The show was sponsored by Quaker Oats, who advertised that their puffed rice and oats were "shot from guns." This was supposed to propel us to the grocery store, as if we, still under the sway of World War II propaganda, would somehow find it patriotic to eat cereal blasted from howitzers.

Given the battles surrounding my relationships with the television and with my father, the idea of the TV shooting back at me with amber bullets of grain launched by a grizzled old man was too much for me to bear. Did Gabby know about the urinal behind the television? Had Gabby wheeled out the guns especially to face *me*—the one who had rebelled against the television deity once too often? Come to think of it, if you shaved off Gabby's beard and left only a pencil-thin moustache, you might just discover my father's face behind the cannons.

When I saw that face and those guns, I shrieked and ran to hide behind the kitchen door. A fortified bunker could be created out of the narrow space between the opened door and the wall. There was my refuge. My brother gleefully called attention to my act of supreme cowardice, as if it enhanced his own bravery in facing the guns. But, small and scared behind that fortress, I knew I was saving my own life. My family laughed at my fear and my tears. I became the sacrificial victim, so they could remain brave. Fear was my domain; I felt that I inhabited it alone.

Sadly, now, I can see my father's face laughing at my fear. There are cruel moments in every child's life, and this was one of mine. Now that I am a father, I know there are moments when I might have found my own small child crying about an imagined fear. I know the moment might have seemed funny, but I also know I needed to treat that fear seriously. Somehow my father never could get around to the second part of that job. He laughed at my tears; I remember that happening a lot. Was he thereby laughing in the face of fear—in my face filled with fear? I can see him making the sign for "cry" and the sign for "baby." I was a baby and I was crying, but to him I was only a crybaby. And I recall my brother in the background, joining the laughter. There, too, my mother, tears in her eyes for the joke of the boy behind the door. When Dickens wrote about childhood humiliation, about Oliver Twist in the coal bin, he well understood the resentment and pain of the small. I raised my fist, like Rastignac at the end of *Père Goriot,* and, without being seen, said to myself, "I'll get you! I'll get even!"

Getting even was easier said than done. Most of the time I remained fairly helpless and fearful. This was fueled by the fact that my father had a somewhat paranoid streak about the world. He warned us all the time against the dangers that lurked beyond our door. That world was filled with murderers, thieves, crackpots, and spoilers—the characters peopling his mind who would take advantage of him. Before leaving the house, my father always mumbled a prayer and kissed the *mezzuzah* on the door in an act of ritual protection. It was a tough world out there and you needed all the magic you could muster. When I was old enough to go out alone, my father told me each time I ventured forth to watch out for thieves, to make sure I crossed the streets safely, to beware of losing anything. I was not allowed to have a key to our apartment until I was fourteen. Although I argued strenuously for a key, my father countered with his reasons. He thought that I was certain to lose my key, and thus some genius of housebreaking would find the key and rob and murder us. I suggested that I wear the key around my neck, but Dad was sure that if I got in a fight with a ruffian, the malefactor surely would use the chain as a garrote and choke me to death. So I remained keyless.

Being without keys, I was frequently locked out of the apartment. We had a primitive electrical signal, installed by a deaf electrician, based on an electro-magnetic relay which tripped when the doorbell was rung.

This Rube Goldberg device made an audible click as the falling electrical contact hit the bottom of the box and completed a circuit that turned on a lightbulb over the door and in the bedroom, and a buzzer under the pillow. If things worked well, and if my parents happened to see the light, I was let in. But if, as happened frequently, the electrical contact was balky and only dropped half-way, then the light would never go on, no matter how many times I rang the bell. I grew very sensitive to the sound of the relay, especially when I heard the sickening half-way clunk that told me that I would be an exile in the hallway for several hours.

This moment for me was one I dreaded—the palpable moment of separation and abandonment that was a direct result of my parents' deafness. I was utterly cut off from them, and I could not even telephone. I used to camp outside the door, a familiar fixture to my neighbors who would say, "Oh, locked out again?" I devised various methods to alert my mother or father, whose footsteps I would hear walking by the door, inches away from me. I took pieces of paper and inserted them under the door, hoping that someone would see the paper with its plaintive messages "Let me in!" or "Help! I'm locked out." I waited breathlessly for my mother to happen by, and then despaired as she passed by the note. Sometimes my father would be asleep in the arm chair by a window that let onto the air shaft. By going up a half-story to the landing just above my floor, and by leaning out the window, I could see him snoring over the *Daily News*. I'd call out, wave frantically, and send paper airplanes in his direction. Occasionally, I caught their attention, but most of the time I ended up having to wait for my brother to come home or for someone to go out. Those were the most wretched times, filled with boredom and hopelessness. In complete desperation, I rang the bell over and over again, even though I knew that the electrical relay was stuck; I pounded on the door and stomped on the door jamb, hoping someone would feel a vibration. Finally, I just collapsed on the cold tile of the hallway and cried. When the door finally opened, it was difficult to feel relieved.

My father's active domain of triumph was race-walking. He began his career in London during a public transportation strike, turning the drudgery of walking to work into a contest, trying to better his time each day. When the strike was over, he decided to enter a race. Here was an area where he could compete with hearing people and win. He was invited to join the Polytechnic Harriers in London during the period depicted in *Chariots of Fire,* and his acceptance onto this prestigious team was no mean feat for a poor, deaf Jew from the slums of Whitechapel. When he came to the United States, he joined the 92nd Street YMHA's team, the Maccabees, and garnered fame in the world of track and field. Our house was filled with medals and trophies. In fact, there were so many that my father had to donate the larger ones to the Y.

I was proud of my father for his accomplishments, particularly his holding of the unofficial American record for twenty-five miles in the 1930s. He was a determined athlete, and his worst qualities became his best in competition. His stubborn narcissism worked well in the dogged world of heel-and-toe racing. I remember accompanying him each Sunday when he trained. We would get up early and take the subway to Macoombs Dam Park, under the shadow of Yankee Stadium. The crew of seasoned race-walkers included Speranza, the man who walked with his head tilted to one side as if it was broken; and Henry Laskau, the young up-and-coming star. There was the communist who never smiled, and the thin black man whose veins bulged on his race-horse legs as he rubbed aromatic, eye-stinging liniment over them. And there was my father's nemesis, a dentist his same age who always finished neck and neck with him. I was greeted warmly by these men, who gave me money and trinkets. Then I sat up on the bleachers, watching them hustle around and around the track. Occasionally I would try to race, perhaps with another young boy, but my father never encouraged me to do so. This was his sport.

Thanksgiving mornings, while other families slept in, my father and I would arise in the dark and journey downtown for the annual City Hall to Coney Island Walking Race. It was not something to miss. In the basement of City Hall, hundreds of men would don their skimpy shorts, legs akimbo, bandaging joints, jostling each other, talking about their times, their injuries, their records. My father would put on his Maccabee tank top and go up to see what his handicap time would be. I was inevitably confused over the idea of handicapping in a race and *being* handicapped: I assumed that my father had special times given to him because he was deaf.

The starting gun resounded with a disarming crack, but my father never heard it. He routinely arranged for a fellow athlete to tap him so he could get off to a good start. The crowd of athletes would explode into a thunder of footfalls which would diminish in volume as they disappeared into the distance. The mists would hover over the Brooklyn Bridge as my father plunged into the unknown, seeming to me the most intrepid traveler.

I would stay behind with an official, whose borrowed glory me feel special, and then we would drive to various checkpoints along the way. The official (with his impressive badge) would make sure each walker always had one foot on the ground, since running was prohibited. I remember standing on Ocean Parkway and watching my father pass by, a handkerchief tied around his hand, so he could wipe his nose efficiently without missing a stride or a drop. He would cast a quick glance at me, never really waving or smiling, intent on his victory.

I was proud of him for being a fine racer, but intensely embarrassed by his lack of clothing. Spectators who lined the street were bundled in their overcoats, protected against the cool autumn air, while he walked briskly past in what appeared to be his underwear. In those days one rarely saw people on the street in athletic clothing, so my father's garb (or lack of it) was extraordinary. Passersby always gaped at the skimpy attire and ungainly walk of the racers, making me feel again the embarrassment that I typically associated with my father appearing in public. In this way race-walking and deafness seemed to coincide.

I would wait by the finish line, at the boardwalk in Coney Island, with the sea behind me, surrounded by strangers. In the distance he would appear, skinny, knobby kneed, all bones and ligaments, striding in that odd hip-swinging way, passing the finish line, often winning the race, and usually winning in his age category. He looked weary, with salt crusted around the corners of his lips. He was in his sixties, his age beginning to show. He would tell me about how he had passed the horrible dentist, or how he taken a wrong turn. I was fascinated. Here my Dad was a famous guy, crowned in glory.

Now, years later, I run. I took up running in my early twenties, far away from my father. My reasons were aesthetic, or so I thought. I had seen a silent film from the 1920s at the Museum of Modern Art, showing some famous runner striding through the Bois de Boulogne, so I thought I'd try. I ran a mile and almost collapsed, but slowly I built up my training regimen until I was running in races. Running seemed different enough from race-walking that I did not feel I had to measure up to my father.

When I entered the first New York City Marathon, in 1976, my father showed up at the finish line. Only six hundred runners entered the race that year. At the finish line I literally ran into my father's arms, crying at the thrill of finishing, and of being my father's son. I had the experience this time of his waiting for me at the finish line and being proud of my athletic accomplishment. This was just a few years before he died.

While writing this recollection, I went one rainy day to a used furniture store in upstate New York. Amid the rows of naugahyde couches and Danish-modern pole lamps, I saw the Emerson console. It was the same model, the exact same. My wife and children were with me, and I called them over as if I had discovered an ancient monolith covered with runes primary to Western culture. The moment was amazing, like the scene in *Citizen Kane* when the camera sweeps along the detritus of Kane's life, the warehouse filled with Kane's possessions, and zooms in on the sled called "Rosebud." Here was my "Rosebud," my madeleine, my golden calf. It sat impassively, like a dethroned idol.

I reached out to open the forbidden gold box, now with the confidence of an adult. There were the four controls, just as I remembered them. Nothing had changed.

3 The Two Mothers

Do you hear the children weeping,
    O my brothers,
Ere the sorrow comes with years?
They are leaning their young heads
    against their mothers,
And that cannot stop their tears.

—Elizabeth Barrett Browning,
    "The Cry of the Children"

My mother died when I was twenty-three and living in Paris. I had a maid's room on the top floor of a comfortable apartment building just off the Boulevard Montparnasse. I was studying with some famous French thinkers: Roland Barthes, Michel Foucault, Jacques Lacan, Claude Lévi-Strauss. It was a heady experience.

I had barely said good-bye to my mother after returning to New York from Central America by way of California. I recall kissing her in September 1972 as I left for the airport for my big year in France. It was heartfelt farewell, although I did not then know I would never see her alive again.

I remember waking up in Paris on the morning of September 29 and saying to my new American girlfriend, "I just had a strange dream. I dreamt about a truck and a hospital or a hotel." A sunny and blonde Coloradan, Susan lay rubbing her eyes and looking at me quizzically as a telegram slid into the room through the mail slot. I walked over, picked it up, opened it, and read its succinct message: "Mother hit by truck. Come home. Gerald."

I slumped down in a numb panic. Susan watched me without quite knowing what to do. I found myself dressed and running down rue de Chevreuse toward Reid Hall, the Columbia University residence in Paris, without knowing how I got out of the apartment. M. Soyer, the concierge, telephoned America for me. I heard my brother's flat, metallic voice. "Mom is in a coma. She'll probably die. She was hit by a truck when she was crossing Second Avenue coming from the Deaf Club. Get home as quickly as you can before she dies."

How I managed to make the arrangements for a flight to New York and to get to the airport I am not sure. But I gave Susan my keys, told her to invite all my friends and have a party to use up my food. On the bus to Orly airport I kept saying over and over again, "Ma mère etait blessée par une camion. Elle va mourir." This mantra of shock got me to the airport and miraculously onto an Air France flight. My one hope was that I could get back in time to touch my mother's living hand.

As I waited for the plane to take off, the pilot announced that the windshield was cracked and that we would have to disembark and wait for three hours. We all filed off the plane.

Then we were told that the windshield actually was not cracked and we should immediately reboard. *Elle va mourir. Ma mère etait blessée.* Once back on the plane, we were informed that the windshield was not reparable and that there would be a substantial delay.

At this point I explained my problem. The attendant helped me find a Greek airliner that was leaving for New York shortly. I retrieved my bags and ran in that frenzied way that one can only run in an airport when a plane is about to be missed. I rushed to the departure gate, only to see the passengers waiting. Flat tires on this plane would involve a substantial delay. As I sat waiting again, I thought of my mother, lying in a coma in New York. I could not get to her.

Somehow that vision seemed to resonate. The separation, though more dramatic, seemed familiar. I had always been separated from her.

At night I could not call her to me, the umbilical cord of sound ruptured between us. Even to this day, when I turn off the light before going to bed, I always experience a panic I now associate with death. In Orly the separation and the death were palpable. I could not touch her because of the distance. Communication was beyond the reach of my fingers. Sign language was stilled.

When I think about my mother, I must think about two mothers: the mother I thought I had when I was a child, and the mother I realized I had when, as an adult, I thought things through. So strong was my need to be loved and cared for that I quilted a mother out of the small, damaged swatches she gave me. The mother I had as a child was affectionate, loving, giving, and attentive. In my battles with my brother and my father, I could turn to her for comfort. Her lap was a safe place. She listened to me, and I could make her laugh so much she would cry. I listened to her tales of her childhood; I went with her on her errands; I learned to cook with her. I always imagined that if I was hurt or wounded, unconscious in a hospital, I would wake to see her face smiling with celestial warmth and feel her caressing touch. Yet, as I look back from an adult distance, she was often and dangerously absent. The vision of radiant sunshine around her face was partially crafted from my own need.

A significant moment in this history of absence occurred when I was knocked unconscious playing baseball. I was standing in front of our apartment building, not paying much attention to the game. A boy swung a bat as I walked into it. I received its blast full in my mouth and fell unconscious onto the ground. My friends abandoned me, feeling that they had done some real harm. As I awoke from my swoon, there was no radiant maternal face there, only my tongue going over my teeth and feeling my gums. Slowly pulling myself off the blood-soaked ground, I cried out, "Mommy!" There was no answer. I dragged myself back to our apartment and to my mother. That long bloodstained march upstairs left a spoor of pain, more from being alone than from physical injury.

My mother was a sweet woman, long suffering the oppression of my father's moods. When I read through the love letters she wrote to my father, I see a strong young woman who had a definite sense of herself and her needs. When my father proposed marriage to her after meeting her only a few times, she was cautious, articulate, and balanced. Over the course of two years she fought the bureaucracy in England and the United States, stood up to my father's hasty importunings, and finally left her family, friends, and world to go to New York and her awaiting lover. But over years she seemed to lose her will, her feistiness. I glimpsed her spirit occasionally when she argued with my father, but more often I saw quiet resignation. Often she was depressed, though we didn't have that word in our lexicon. Her world had shrunk, I think, from the athletic, trip-taking, tight community of young deaf people she knew to the once-a-week visit to the Deaf Club in New York; from the nuclear family with her many sisters and brothers to the one-bedroom apartment and the fragmented extended family in the United States. She worked hard, taking in sewing at home, altering clothing in a department store, raising two boys. But her life lacked fun or adventure. And she was living with a man who was darkly sullen half the time and angry the other half, with occasional bouts of humor between.

I worked hard at being the light in her life. She and I talked a great deal. It was from her that I learned to talk to women. We would sit together, when there was time, and just chat. Her hands would tell me stories, convey feelings, forge the bond between us by making signs in the air. She was often the one with whom I played games when I was lonely. I cooked with her and helped her clean the house. This simple togetherness gave me a love of the domestic, the mundane.

But I remember quickly outgrowing her intellectually. She did not have the need to seek out much beyond her sphere. My father aimed, through his race-walking, to defy the way hearing people perceived him; he also enjoyed acting in and writing plays for the Deaf Club. My mother seemed content to be a housewife. Perhaps because her speech was better than his, she did not so much seek the approval of hearing people.

My mother never read novels; she rarely watched television; she almost never read the newspaper. She toiled and drudged her way through life, her pleasure her friends and her children. She enjoyed dressing up to go to the Deaf Club, and she enjoyed the captioned films they showed there. I am not really sure how my mother spent her time at home. She vacuumed only once every few weeks and was not a compulsive cleaner. The apartment was always neat, although a thin layer of dust often coated the mahogany furniture. Time just seemed to melt into silence. She was as close to a Zen Buddhist as you could find in the Bronx, surrounded by an aura of quietude.

She did, however, cook all the meals we ate—for better or worse. Her culinary tastes were formed by the unfortunate confluence of Jewish and English cuisines. She koshered all her meat at home, a laborious process that involved sprinkling coarse salt on slabs of tough meat and then washing them repeatedly, until what little flavor and blood had resided in the animal were exorcised in rivulets that ran down the drain. Then she would boil or pressure cook the item and finally sprinkle a little paprika on it to reinstill flavor. It was a revelation when I discovered the existence of spices other than salt, pepper, and paprika.

I learned to cook by watching my mother and by viewing television cooking shows; the latter gave me a sense of grandeur and comfort that my home lacked. While Julia Child and her ilk would whip up a cassoulet, my mother would chop liver. Like many deaf people who attended residential schools, my mother always made the same meal on the same night of the week. Potatoes and sour cream (not a side dish but the entree) on Monday. Omelets and mashed potatoes on Tuesday. (No meal was complete without a potato, my father revering that tuber over all other vegetables.) Wednesday, pot roast; Thursday, fried fish with french fries. Friday night we had chicken, of course, and Saturday afternoon she always prepared "chicken chow mein"—Minute Rice with chopped-up bits of chicken, all mixed up with ketchup and sprinkled over crispy Chinese noodles. Sunday night's offering was spaghetti with butter and ketchup, sometimes refried the following day for lunch or supper. The menu rarely varied, although the occasional substitution of stuffed cabbage was possible. The only green vegetable we ever had was canned peas. Frozen food was looked upon as alien; besides, our refrigerator was too small to keep anything frozen. I never saw a green salad in my childhood. Dessert was usually canned fruit, particularly Del Monte's fruit cocktail, whose Red Dye #2 cherry I would claim for my cancerous own.

When I look back on this selection now, it seems barbarous. But I loved it then, as did my father and brother. My wife, who is Italian American, still cannot get over the spaghetti with butter and ketchup; nevertheless, for years after I learned to prepare crepes and mousses, I would guiltily prepare that childhood entree for myself. As did my brother. The only meal that survives in my current repertoire is salmon cutlets, which must be served with French dressing, mashed potatoes, and green peas. An amazingly comforting meal.

Mother could only understand little parts of me. Because I needed her so much, I tried to only show her the parts she understood. Her wish was that I would be a "nice boy": clean, cute, well behaved, and conforming to normal standards. Of course, I was not only that: I was also dirty, rebellious, and stubborn. Because she could not comprehend my noncompliant self, and because I could not bear the rejection of that part of me, I agreed not to reveal it, and she agreed not to see it. This turned out to be a bad deal in the long run. When I used to ask her, hopefully, if she loved me, she always had the same reply: "Yes, but you are so stubborn."

I recall a very early dream in which I was trapped in a glass bottle by a witch. I tried to jump up and push the cork out of the bottle, but I was too small. So I got a corkscrew and pushed into the cork, turning it from inside the bottle, but in a way that the cork was forced out. The feeling of being trapped and alone, having to solve problems for myself, was an apt metaphor for my life within my family. Although my memory of my mother was benign, I must have recognized that she was the witch I could not let myself call wicked. And the corkscrew speaks for itself.

My early memories of my mother are suffused with the smell of wool and Prell shampoo, of my small head on her shoulder. Even now, whenever I press my nose to wool, I enter a world of remembrance. I used to sniff Prell the way a lover savors the perfume of the first night. Mediating between the danger of the dark and the abandonment of the deaf ear was the pleasure of being held against the wool and near the scented hair. There I could be felt and seen, if not heard. There I could be safe.

Strangely, the smell of Ivory soap depresses me beyond words. So do ceiling lights. Were there hot summer days when I was plunged, screaming, into soapy bath water? Ceiling lights and Ivory soap remind me of the unremittingly dreary, hot days of summer in the Bronx. The sun became unbearable as it intensified the heat and glare of the yellow bricks.

Sometimes my mother got me up early, when the city still held traces of the night's cool touch, and we journeyed an hour-and-a-half trek by bus to Orchard Beach. These rare trips recalled those of my mother's youth, when she and her deaf friends would take excursions to the ocean. Orchard Beach was the only beach I ever knew, except for occasional outings to Brighton Beach, where the deaf used to congregate around the tall poles announcing numbered sections. Going to the beach was one of the only experiences I ever shared with my mother alone, other than to shop or stay home. We never brought anything along except towels and lunch. My mother always packed sliced cucumbers. I cooled my hot lips on those slices, even if the cucumbers were coated with sand, and felt that my mother had provided me some physical comfort.

Protection was only partial. We never had an umbrella because we had no car in which to transport one, and of course renting an umbrella was an unthinkable luxury. So we inevitably baked in the sun, rubbed useless pre-PABA Coppertone on our bodies, and came home roasted. Lying in bed at night was an agony matched only by the close heat of summer trapped in the stale apartment buildings.

Orchard Beach—"Horse Shit Beach," as we kids jocularly called it—must have been attractive at one time. By the 1950s it bore all the hallmarks of institutions for the working classes. The bus stop had long mazes of metal railings to channel the thousands of carless beach-goers in orderly lines as they waited for the exhaust-spewing buses to take them back to the tenements. The bathrooms at the beach reeked of urine, and there was a repulsive, perpetual wetness on their slimy tiles. The coastline was divided into numbered sections, so that we could say to the Zuckermans, "Meet you at section 8." It never occurred to me that it was strange to number a beach. The sand was a minefield of detritus; garbage of every kind could be sifted up with a casual kick of the foot. Nedicks containers, Good Humor ice cream cups, paper napkins, popsicle sticks were easily recycled into toys. The sand was territorially colonized by families whose domain ended where the next blanket or towel began. Often there was no room to see the sand. The water was always a brackish yellow.

Orchard Beach had virtually no waves because it faced Long Island Sound. These still waters ran deep and dirty. I would often hear about the breakers at Jones Beach: "Six feet high," my friend Victor Morabito would brag, since his family had a car. I longed to go there and feel the power of the surf, to hear Guy Lombardo playing under the stars. But since my parents were deaf and never learned to drive, we had no car. This consigned us to the lapping urine of Orchard Beach.

My mother and I generally arrived early and made a pretense of heading out to an area where there were fewer people. Within minutes that place, too, would have become settled by hundreds of others seeking solitude. To avoid them you could go still further out, but what was the point? Others would just come later. The aim was to swim, dig, and run around. My mother did almost nothing on the beach, as I recall. She didn't read. She couldn't swim. She would sit on the towel, close her eyes, and lie down. Then she would arise and dutifully go down to the sea, tap some water on her shoulders, to avoid a shock to the system, before slowly lowering herself into the waters. There she would squat and let the polluted waters lap around her bathing suit, with its little undulating skirt. That was enough.

Then somehow it was lunch time. We would ate our egg-salad sandwiches, cucumber slices, and Good Humor ice cream. Then I had to wait the excruciating hour or two after eating to avoid the dreaded cramp that no one ever got. And then, after building some sand castles and destroying the outer layers of my epidermis as the sun raged down on me, I was permitted to return to the waveless waters for additional saline and urine therapy. Finally my mother would tell me that I should put on a T-shirt because my skin looked red. Then we prepared to wait in the metal mazes for an hour until an empty city bus appeared. These lugubrious vehicles lurched and stopped, taking us through unfamiliar neighborhoods, many with green trees and wide avenues unlike our own. Eventually we could see the small, cramped streets lined with low yellow buildings, could feel the oppressive closeness of the heat. We knew we were home.

Those days I spent with my mother were quiet, almost empty, but strangely satisfying. The pleasure was the kind that a dog gets from sitting next to a warm body. My mind began to develop and fill with strange images, odd conclusions, swervy perspectives. There was no one with whom I could share these. My brother would torture me into submission; my father was asleep on the couch with the *Daily News* on his lap; my mother would never understand. I remember thinking about the 7-Up bottle that said "You like it; it likes you." I would spend hours thinking about the palindromal aspects of that phrase. *How* did it like me? I did like it. Wasn't it amazing? I knew I could never share this linguistic delight with my mother. She would just say, "Silly, think too much. Eat up."

I would wander around the house and say I was bored. My mother gave me columns of numbers to add up. This was her idea of occupying me. Oddly enough, I looked forward to these adventures in pre-accounting. When I could get her momentarily to stop cleaning the house or preparing food, I asked her to tell me stories. But she was often unstoppable. I would lie in her way on the living room floor, pretending to be dead, and she would vacuum around me. I would leap up and sign furiously, "What if I really dead? You not even notice!" She would laugh and say, "Can tell you not really dead." But I would try next time to look really dead. It never worked.

I tried to get her to tell me stories about her own life. Her past vital self came back then, like a ghost haunting an empty house. She told me of how she became deaf—a story I could not hear too often. She told me about her life in Liverpool—about her parents' house, the preparations for Passover. How she slept with her two other sisters in one bed, and how each would try to fluff over to herself the meager allotment of feathers stuffed in the quilt. She told me about her fear of Asians after she saw a silent movie about English women being kidnapped as white slaves for some Chinese whoremonger, and how, as a child, she never went to the Chinese laundry without quaking. She told me about going to the ocean—not Orchard Beach, but some island near Liverpool that could be reached only at low tide. She and her friends spent the day on the island and then return home at night. Of course, one night she almost missed low tide and risked being stranded. Somehow she got off the island, but I can't remember how.

I loved her stories and made her tell them over and over. I never understand how the slim, athletic, tanned, buxom young brunette who formed the apex of a pyramid of deaf men and women (as I had seen in photographs) turned into the quiet, patient, out-of-shape Griselda of a housewife.

Nor could I understand why she married my father, who seemed to spend much of his life telling her what she was doing wrong. That was the great subject of interest to me. My mother told me of a rich suitor, Isadore Alpers from Leeds, also deaf, who had wooed her in England. This was when she was corresponding with my father in America, and they already had an understanding that she would marry him. At one crucial point, my mother broke off the relationship and began seeing this rich suitor. Eventually she decided in favor of my father. I always wondered what would have happened had she chosen this fellow from Leeds. She would have been rich, instead of living in a tenement in the

South Bronx. And I would not have been born. Sometimes, when I was especially infuriated at my father, I wished she had married the rich suitor anyway, just so she would have had a husband who was not so moody and difficult.

When my mother arrived in America and was about to be married, there was a moment to which she always referred with some sadness and resignation. She and my father were boarding a bus in Manhattan. He was in one of his impatient moods, and he yelled at her to hurry up and sit down. She began to cry, unused to such gruff treatment. She felt the enormity of having crossed the Atlantic to marry a man who would treat her so rudely. I remember that conversation because my mother rationalized it all by saying, "But he is a good man, works hard, never beats me." Even at my young age, I thought this was not a good enough reason to be married.

I often wondered whether my parents loved each other. My father frequently treated my mother with hostility and contempt, as he did my brother and me, but he was also an affectionate man who was capable of adoration and love. My mother seemed to have a quiet resignation toward my father. I always sensed that she felt she could have loved someone else better. But, like my father, she was a stoic. Having experienced the abuses of the hearing world, my parents had learned to tolerate a high level of disappointment and frustration. My father said he loved my mother; she said she loved him; they both said they loved my brother and me. Yet I never really was convinced about any of it.

I loved my mother with the desperation of a loving heart that needs an object. She was often my playmate, especially when I was young. She used to sing to me in her flat, uninflected voice. The only song she knew was "Christmas is a' coming," which I supposed she learned at school before she became deaf, despite her being Jewish. I used to try to get her to sing in tune by instructing her to sing higher or lower, but she would only sing more loudly or softly.

We used to play checkers together. But I hated to lose, and if I lost, I cried. Unlike my other playmates, she often arranged things so that I would win—but then I cried because she lost on purpose. She told me to be a good sport. I never was.

As I learned about the world in school and by reading, I gladly became my mother's teacher. She was strangely ignorant of the world. For example, she did not believe that the moon or the planets were real. She knew they were in the sky, but she thought of them as illusory. This was a belief to which she firmly adhered, despite my use of photographs and other scientific sources to the contrary. Being with her was like living in a previous century. After her father died, I recall her asking me, "Why do people have to die?" I answered with ten-year-old authority, telling her about the population explosion and how the old must make way for the new. I could see that she found this logic comforting, even though I still ask myself the same question without gaining the satisfaction of the same comfort.

What my mother did try to teach me was the morality of the working class. She was no revolutionary. Rather, she had ingested the work ethic completely. She wanted me to be good, compliant, cooperative, and above all unselfish. As a deaf woman, she had learned by hard experience to tolerate all kinds of abuses; and as a working woman, more so.

When I was a child she used to take in alterations at home. I would peek into the living room and see women in various stages of undress, my mother hunched at their feet, pins in her mouth, tape measure over her shoulder, marking the darts, pleats, and hems that would turn these Bronx maidens into Lana Turners or Doris Days. I enjoyed the prurient voyeurism of watching Miss Bloch, the instructor at the Arthur Murray Dance Studio, strip down to her black underwear. However, I was embarrassed by and resented my mother's scuttling around on her knees. I was also abashed but secretly pleased to accept the money (that I was taught to always refuse at first) that these women slipped into my hands, alms for the son of the poor seamstress. My mother never expressed resentment toward her clients. They provided her livelihood, and she was always proud of her work.

When I was older, my mother went to work at Franklin Simon, a department store near Macy's. Although the store's public areas were rather luxurious, the alterations department was located in a cramped, stifling room filled with steam from the pressing machine, abuzz with the whirring and groaning of the sewing machines. My mother sat contentedly in this squalor, her reading glasses on the tip of her nose, always friendly with her colleagues, a benign presence. Her survival skill of silent resignation was one she wanted me to learn. One of her favorite phrases, after "Don't cry over spilt milk," was "Don't be a dog in the manger." Anytime I wanted anything, the dog would appear in the manger. I never really understood what a manger was, but I knew I wanted to sit in it even if the damned horse died.

"Don't be selfish," both my father and mother demanded. But being selfish meant defining a self, saying no, fighting an injustice. So I always was selfish, while feeling I should not be.

My mother took me few places besides the daily round of shopping and visiting relatives or friends, but once we rode the subway to Madison Square Garden, where the Ringling Brothers brought their annual extravaganza. I am not sure what prompted her to take me to the circus, since outings for personal pleasure were almost nonexistent. I think perhaps I suggested it. I cannot imagine she said to herself, "The circus is in town. I'll take Lenny."

I thought I would adore the circus, but when we arrived at the cavernous building thronged with children and smelling of sawdust and manure, I wasn't so sure. Our seats were the least expensive, of course, and so far back that I could barely see anything. Also, since Ringling Brothers was a three-ring circus, and since I was so excited, I could not bring myself to concentrate on any one ring, so I remained visually confused through most of the experience. My mother could not hear the ringmaster's announcements telling who was in which ring and so could not clarify anything for me. I was just a small boy sitting in a vast space, staring occasionally at blobs of light far below. At that time the circus sold small flashlights suspended on lanyards that could be swung around one's head. The effect of thousands of small children swinging their penlights over their heads was impressive. The cavernous darkness glittered with twinkling lights like the starry void itself. In desperation at my own confusion, I whirled my flashlight around more and more vigorously, joining my light with the anonymous others, all the while feeling guilty for having forced my mother to pay for the beautiful but useless flashlight and for not understanding what was going on.

One memory I do have is of the Flying Wallendas, who were shot out of (fake) cannons. Men in capes and women wearing barely anything became human projectiles launched in rapid succession, reminding me of Gabby Hayes's puffed rice being shot from guns. I aspired to be a Wallenda, with a helmet and cape that would transform me into a human bullet. I practiced at home, trying to shoot myself up from the springs of my bed, accompanied by drum rolls and imagined puffs of smoke and flashes of light. I desperately wanted to be famous, to make my mark, to be heard and recognized as something more than the smart child of deaf parents.

The worst part of the circus was the sideshow. My mother took me to the midway to see "the freaks." It was another incredible act of misjudgment to bring a child my age to witness the impairments of others. Perhaps to adults this display was just an interesting diversion, but to me it was an absolute chamber of horrors. I recall seeing the giant, a man with acromegaly. The sideshow barker praised his strength, but it seemed that his physical difference, rather than being glorious (as the barker said), was a form of sadness bred into the body. There was an armless woman who could type with her toes and light a cigarette with her feet. The crescendo of physical differences built up through a bearded woman to, at last, the woman with elephant skin. She sat in her cubicle as the crowd strained to see her. She was holding a box of Kleenex and crying softly to herself as the barker described her special traits. To me she looked like a distraught woman with a disfiguring skin disease. Throughout this show of horrors my mother remained next to me, observant but impassive. Did she ever connect her own invisible deafness with these? "Ladies and gentlemen, the deaf woman! This amazing lady can talk by observing your lips alone. Yes, and she speaks a language entirely with her fingers. Go ahead, Eva, show the people how you can talk with your hands! And when she speaks, she sounds like a trained seal!"

I must have recognized this sideshow parallel to my own life. I felt so sad and uncomfortable, seeing with a child's clear vision that these were people with disabilities or differences, who were only in their extremity compelled to show their impairments to the public.

By the time we came to the muscle man, I was nervous and depressed. Feelings of overwhelming claustrophobia began to rise in me as I was shoved along in this pushing, gawking mass of adults and children. The muscle man's hand came down and smashed a two-by-four. At exactly that moment a girl my age, perhaps upset the way I was, fell on me in a faint. As she did, I screamed, turned around, and pushed my way through the crowd in a panic. I fought my way through the bodies, the thoughtless boys, the insensitive adults, the indifferent flesh of an oblivious world. I was lost momentarily, without my mother. When she found me crying and gasping for breath, she asked me what happened. I believe I said, "Too crowded." No point in explaining.

When I have these thoughts, I feel the guilt of betrayal. I should be dwelling on the mother I thought I had in my childhood, not the one I came to know after she died. My job in life was to make my parents feel adequate, competent, fulfilled. They gave me life, and out of guilt and thanks I had to give life back to them. Or was their job to take life away from the real me, to substitute a nice boy who behaved and was clean and unselfish? If my parents, both dead now, could ever have read these thoughts, they would have been disappointed. It is an ultimate irony that for me to explain myself in writing is to define a person my parents never knew or even could know. They were undereducated for this task, by a system that saw them as freaks, and a class and an era that underestimated the inner lives of children.

Much of what I remember about my mother had to do with shopping. I see myself hanging onto her flowered tapestry handbag with the wooden handles. We often descended the dingy marble stairs of the apartment building together, my mother somewhat dressed up and always her dark red lipstick applied with a flourish and blotted with toilet paper into maroon lip-prints that ended up floating in the toilet like exotic camellias. We passed by the apartment buildings on Clinton Avenue, walking past the always drunk man on the steps of one, and traversed the long block to the main shopping thoroughfare.

On Tremont Avenue stores were crowded together in a comforting confusion. The trolley car wires hung suspended in the air like tightrope nets; with the streetcar tracks embedded in the cobblestones of the avenue below, they created a visual chaos that seemed appropriately to echo the disorder of the stores and the people. This was the era when housewives addressed each other as Mrs. Zuckerman or Mrs. Davis, in keeping with the Old World dignity they had brought with them across the Atlantic. My mother would nod or say hello to various women. These acknowledgments always amazed me, because my own acquaintances did not extend much past my block. Since my domain was so small, I assumed that my mother's knowledge of people could not be much greater. I would always ask her if she knew the person to whom she had bid hello, and she would respond saying that she knew them by sight. This kind of acquaintance mystified me, particularly because of my mother's deafness. How could she know people whom I did not know?

There were times I fought with my mother on Tremont Avenue. Then she did the thing that I hated most: she asserted her adulthood over my childhood. I would be crying, and she would say, "All right, if you won't come with me, then good-bye." The relationship between the two of us was so much more complicated than between hearing parents and children. True, I was a child; but I was also the one she had to ask about the hearing world. I interpreted for her. I heard what she could not hear, and I knew more about that world, in some respects, than did she. So I hated it when she took away the independence that she had ceded to me. I watched her as she walked off, her image growing smaller and smaller as she passed by the shops and the shoppers, until finally I had to acknowledge my own helplessness and run to her crying against my will. I was forced, because of circumstance, to be independent when my mother was present; when left alone, I was forced to see how dependent I was. In either case, I lost.

Johnnie's, the produce store, was an alluring and sinister place peopled by tough-looking Italian men, their T-shirt sleeves rolled up, their hair greased back and falling in curls over their foreheads. They smoked Camels and talked to my mother fresh and flirty. "What'll it be, doll?" "These tomatoes are really soft, honey—jus' like you." I had to interpret and tell her the tomatoes were soft, but I didn't include the insinuating endearments. I felt I had to protect her from something I sensed but could not articulate, from the men who called familiarly about ripe tomatoes. What were such tough men doing feeling fruit and praising its juicy sweetness on a hot summer afternoon in the Bronx?

The stores on Tremont Avenue seemed to be extensions of my domestic space. Each one had sensory memories that I associate with my mother. On the corner was the delicatessen. From its counter, which was like a bar complete with a brass footrest, came the deeply dark smell of cured meats, the tang of frankfurters, with the steaming background scent of hot knishes on the griddle. You could stay there and eat, but for a Sunday afternoon lunch we preferred to take the food home. Perhaps because my parents wanted to keep their deafness to themselves, we rarely ate out. As I grew older it was my job to go and buy this lunch. The assignment was pleasant, but it interrupted "The Jewish Hour" on the radio, hosted by Rabbi Balfour Brickner. I hated to miss the program's songs, stories, and dramas, so I took my transistor radio (in those days a quite large but new invention) with my ear plug concealed under my earmuffs (which I wore in summer or winter: better for passersby to think of me as eccentric than to view me as deaf), and wandered down the streets with tales of Chelm in my ears and corned beef in my hands.

Next to the delicatessen was the "appetizing store." There were barrels of pickles, crocks of pickled herring and gefilte fish, walls piled high with jars of assorted candies, mostly the disgusting kind with the soft centers. There one found lox and smoked fish, expertly carved by men with European accents and fat fingers. They would slice the lox with those fingers so thinly that it did not seem possible the work was done by human hands. I would watch as my mother ordered the foods that I abhorred—fish of all names from around the world, kippers and the golden-skinned whitefish, tinned sardines whose mermaid tails would disappear down my parents' throats as if they were imitating the feats of sea lions at feeding time. My parents specialized in eating foods that would repulse the palate of any normal child: chicken feet, chicken fat, tongue, bone marrow, stuffed derma, boiled chicken necks, schmaltz herring, and more. They were bottom feeders as a result of centuries of life in the Polish *shtetls* where our ancestors ate the bread of human affliction and the pickles of peasant oppression.

Down the street was Stein's Kosher Butcher Shop. It seemed I spent hours there because my mother knew Mr. and Mrs. Stein. My job was to interpret as Mr. Stein would say, "Tell your mother, I got a beautiful piece of flanken for her," as he held up a large red slab of meat and slapped its side as if it were the derriere of Marilyn Monroe. I always associated sex with the butcher because there were full-color advertising posters for lamb that featured sexy cowgirls with red bandannas around their necks, seductively holding baby lambs and smiling out at me. As I sat on the pine bench and kicked the sawdust with my feet, I would gaze into the cowgirl's deep blue eyes and think of lamb chops. Meanwhile, my mother would pluck her own chicken and singe off its pin feathers over a gas jet in the back of the butcher store, where rites of the flesh were performed daily.

There was a store that sold live pigeons. The window was filled with pigeons of every color and kind; because they perched there, the glass was so discolored that you could barely see in. If you pressed your face against the blotchy window, you could see a visual cacophony of wings, heads, legs, and feathers. Inside the store Italian men sat on crates, amidst still more crates filled with pigeons. A bare light bulb illuminated the store, and cigarette smoke filled the air with haze. Men in my neighborhood raised pigeons on their roofs, just like Marlon Brando in *On the*

Waterfront. Once or twice a day the owners would open the door of the coop and release the birds, but the pigeons never seemed to want to fly. The man in his T-shirt would force them out by waving a stick with a piece of cloth on the end. The flocks would circle the roof and then immediately return to their perches, as if they thought flying was a bad idea when you came right down to it. The men who raised pigeons looked like the men who sold produce. It was always strange to me why they loved pigeons, these men who appeared so sinister and criminal, clones of Jimmy Cagney or Richard Widmark. But, while their cigarettes dangled from their lips, they would hold the birds and stroke their iridescent necks like fond lovers.

A store opened on Tremont Avenue that I now realize foretold the demise of the traditional shops, the end of the stores that captured the essence of my mother and the Old World ways. This embodiment of the new was called the "I Can Sell It Wholesale Store," but it was immediately dubbed "Cheap Charley's" and that name stuck. This store, a pint-sized forerunner of Kmart, had a little bit of everything in odd lots at reduced prices. Mainly my friends and I stole from it—or "copped" things, as we renamed our activity, to make it seem less criminal. The major item we copped was the "spaldeen," a pink rubber ball made by Spaulding. We needed spaldeens to play many of our street games. One of us would enter the store and try to look invisible; others would stand in front of the store on guard; still others would try distract the owners. At the crucial moment a spaldeen would go into someone's pocket and the rest of us would run as fast as we could. I never liked copping things, and I tried to stay on the periphery of the action. Afterward I would talk about how "we" had copped the ball.

As I associate my mother with the neighborhood, I also link her in my mind to the apartment building in which we lived. It was a five-story walk-up made of the loathsome yellow brick that will forever haunt the palette of my mind. Piss yellow, pus yellow, aged newspaper yellow. The apartments were one and two bedroom, as if there were no greater expectations of family increase. There was a buzzer system to let you into the building, but when it broke, it was never repaired. The door was simply left unlocked. The interior hallway was small and tiled, with mailboxes in the dark recess under the staircase. The hallway always felt dark and dank—in the hot summers a not completely unwelcome feeling, since air conditioning was scarce.

My mother had hearing friends in our apartment building, although my father did not. On the first floor lived Mrs. Bonwit, a neatly dressed old lady who always wore formal-looking clothing and kept her thinning hair in the style of the 1930s. A thin layer of powder coated her aging face, and deep red lipstick melted into the cracks of her upper lip. She was frozen in time, and her apartment was a virtual museum honoring the art deco period. Mr. Bonwit had died some years ago in the bedroom; she never slept there again, keeping the same linens and the bedspread in perpetual homage to his memory. Her grandson Steven would come over to visit and play with me sometimes. I recall he was very good with the hula hoop. He would demonstrate his unusual capacity while my mother and Mrs. Bonwit would sit and discuss their favorite subjects—disease and death. They would go through all the cases of cancer (mentioned with a lowered voice by Mrs. Bonwit), work their way through heart disease, and even more guardedly discuss "women's problems." They talked about the other neighbors. My mother's speech was good enough for most people to understand, and she could lip read well enough. And of course I was always there to help out in interpreting some ailments or horrible symptoms.

"Tell her Mrs. Zuckerman's bladder is infected," my mother would say, and I would dutifully convey the message.

"Tell her that's a shame," Mrs. Bonwit would fire back, and I would toss the comment along to my mother posthaste, all the while trying to match Steven's hula hoop skills.

The other woman with whom my mother was friendly was Ruth Zuckerman. The Zuckermans lived on our floor. Nathan Zuckerman, her husband, was a podiatrist whose office was a block away from our apartment building. Ruth Zuckerman was a sometime piano teacher. They had two children closer to my brother's age, Gerald (known as "Little Gerald" in deference to my brother) and Judy. The Zuckermans were a fascinating family to me. There was something bohemian and unconventional about them: their house was always in disarray; Mr. Zuckerman would walk around in his undershorts; the children referred to their parents by first names.

It was one of my special pleasures to go to Mr. Zuckerman's office. Like many men in my life, Zuckerman was a surrogate father who (unlike my actual father) knew the world. I was continually amazed at other people's parents. Their normality made them seem like geniuses to me. They could drive cars, fix things, order deliveries over the telephone, and even talk to someone in another room.

Zuckerman's office was an apartment on Prospect Avenue. The waiting room was obviously a converted living room. The podiatric office was in the connecting bedroom, separated only by double glass doors hung with curtains; it contained an adjustable barber shop chair. Tired old people, mainly women, would sit in the waiting room, overcome by their own foot-concerned torpors, while Zuckerman worked on one of their compatriots. My job was to bring in basins of hot water in which they would soak their feet. I don't know if they minded my standing by and watching Dr. Zuckerman gouge out their bunions and abrade their calluses; he certainly never asked them. He good-naturedly called me his assistant. People would wince and squirm in the chair as Zuckerman wheezed over them and performed primitive maneuvers that would have made medieval barbers shiver. He had sharp tools, blunt ones, and every form of scalpel known. He would dig into bulbous growths with metal gouges, scooping out fleshy pulp, and the old ladies would howl in pain. People would hobble in and hobble out. I saw every foot deformity imaginable. This was quite an education for a young child, and it discouraged me from ever wanting to become a doctor.

However, the real beauty of Dr. Zuckerman's office was to be found not in the torture room but in the spaces that would have been the kitchen and the rear bedrooms. That was where he and I really spent our best time, for his true interest was not chiropody but electronics. These rooms were filled with every kind of electronic equipment ever built. Oscilloscopes, transformers, tuners, speakers, Van de Graaff generators, every type of dial and knob then known: all were piled one on top of another so that no bit of wall showed. These rooms were like a mad scientist's laboratory, and I was the sorcerer's apprentice. I would come here after school and work on my science projects. If I had nothing else to do, I would just turn on everything so that sine curves were sinuously undulating on twenty different screens while electronic beeps squealed out in differing decibel and tone levels as lightning bolts shot off the top of metal balls. Between bunions, Dr. Zuckerman would come back and examine what I was up to, teach me something new, or help me build model airplanes that could fly by remote control. Mainly I just watched him run around, moving devices from one room to the other, and got lessons in things I did not really have a prayer of understanding. For me, the attention and contact with the older man who knew things was enough. He was my Aristotle, my Leonardo, in a world that seemed devoid of knowledge.

Mrs. Zuckerman was an artiste. She played the piano in her youth and claimed she could have been a concert pianist, but something stopped her. I remember being told that her hands were featured in a movie: some star sat and rhapsodized at the piano, but the closeup revealed not the star's hands but those of Mrs. Zuckerman. The fact that she played the piano at all was a cause for much wonderment and adulation in our not only tone-deaf but stone-deaf family. We treated anyone who played any instrument whatsoever as a latter-day Mozart. (To this day I am impressed when kids play "Chopsticks.") Mrs. Zuckerman would awe me when she launched into "Moonlight Sonata." I would sit at her feet, amidst the discarded *Popular Science* magazines and the curls of dog hair, thinking I was in some European salon. When I was very young, I remember someone rang our doorbell by mistake, looking for Mrs. Zuckerman. I answered the door. It was a man who wanted to know where "the pianist" lived. I had never heard the term, since my parents' vocabulary did not include many words relating to the musical arts. It sounded as if he were asking for "the penis," and I began laughing hysterically. Later, of course, humiliation replaced hilarity as I realized my own deficit.

A Latino family moved into the building next door to us, much to my mother's horror. She was quietly racist, tolerating blacks while subtly stereotyping them with undesirable attributes. But with Latinos, who were rapidly immigrating to the Bronx in the late fifties and early sixties, my mother was not so subtle. The deaf sign at that time for Puerto Rican was a sign for the letter "P" made on the nose and then followed by a slide down and and forward, turning the letter into an "R." Though the sign is rather neutral in its acronymic discretion, it can be and was turned pejorative by its proximity to the nose and a slightly sour look on the face. To her, Puerto Ricans were dirty and lived unwholesome lives. She did not want to live just across the dumb-waiter shaft from them. To confirm her worst feelings, a very large family lived in a one-bedroom unit even smaller than ours (since the living room and kitchen were combined). Salsa music, spicy food aromas, and babies' legs spewed from the apartment every time their door opened. Safaris of cockroaches would file across the few inches that separated their door from ours. My mother was disgusted. When they moved out one night without paying the rent, her worst prejudices were confirmed.

A few other families were significant in our building. Sidney Hoenig and his wife lived on the third floor. He was a math teacher at De Witt Clinton High School, which I eventually attended. He was a youngish, balding, nerdy man with horn-rimmed glasses; his nerdy wife wore harlequin glasses and kept her long hair piled up on her head. They had cats but no children. Childlessness was a severe crime in our neighborhood, met with pity, hostility, or both.

Sidney took an interest in me. We would sit on the steps of the apartment building and discuss things; I can't remember what, but it felt like philosophy. It was he who first told me that the whole was greater than the sum of its parts. As with Zuckerman and the electronics, I didn't really understand what that meant, but I did understand that this was something worth understanding; if not now, then some day. Sidney told me to question authority, saying, "Just because it is in a book doesn't mean that it is right. Just because your teacher says something, doesn't mean it is right." Since he was a teacher, I suppose he knew. Sidney planted in me the idea of being a gadfly.

The fathers in the building were mercurial presences. We saw the mothers all the time, but the fathers were swarthy, tired men who wore sleeveless T-shirts and sat at the kitchen table at night, waiting for supper. They were wordless and threatening in their darkness and unshavenness. They were men whose hands might go up suddenly, drawn back and threatening to hit. They were humorless, drudging in their jobs, spending the weekends drinking beer and playing pinochle, peppering their few utterances with obscenities. I never liked any of them, and I knew to avoid them. What they thought of me, the smart son of the deaf people downstairs, I do not know, but there was mutual suspicion.

My world was with the women, with the mothers. I sat with my mother and listened to her talk, interpreting when necessary. The conversations were boring but suggestive. When I asked for details, I was always denied. "What's the matter?" I would ask. My mother would parry, "Women's problems." "What does that mean?" I would persist. She would point to her womb and make a face that meant trouble. Adultery, divorce, scandal—that was the trade of the women. I tried to listen between the lines, but I never got very far. I was left with the desire to know.

Sometimes when we could not go to the beach, we went on the roof. The roof was a place of wonder. (I felt deeply the free breathing described in Carol King's song "Up on the Roof.") From there the sky was unobstructed. You could see the Empire State Building, even though you were in the Bronx, and the water towers created the impression of a spired, medieval city. My mother and I used to sunbathe, and other tenants would bring up chairs or lie on towels on nice days. The smell of the tarred roof, absorbing the baking rays of the sun in its black, resinous surface, combined with the scent of coconut suntan lotion, Nedicks orange drink, and beer to turn this strange wasteland into a penthouse country club. In the distance the pigeons in their coops would coo and flutter; the cars would honk below. These were the rare moments of transformation, in which the grate and clang of the ordinary became grace notes in a symphony of ease, peace, and satisfaction. It was then that I forgot my humiliations and shame, my relegation to the stark working-class world, and became a vibrant child amid the fullness of the living moment.

My mother was rarely able to protect me from the hearing world. One of my strongest recollections of this occurred one day when I was six and playing on the street. A boy I had never seen before (or since) hit Jill, a girl in our building. It was one of those random, unmotivated crimes that puzzle the mind. Jill's mother (a kind of Neanderthal Valkyrie) was looking out the window from the fifth floor; witnessing the pummeling of her daughter, she gave vent to a banshee-like cry at the offending boy. He dared the Fates by telling her to fuck off. We all looked at each other with admiration and fear for this kind of hubris. The apartment building seemed to shake as Jill's mother ran down the five stairways. We looked at the boy in sympathy, all the while murmuring in vague anticipation, "Are you going to get it."

Jill's mother burst forth from the front of the apartment building like a hellhound and headed screaming directly to—me! Apparently her bad eyesight, combined with certain physical similarities between the boy and me, led her to conclude that I was the villain who had hit her daughter and cursed at her. In one brief instant I realized for the first time the full nature of injustice. I was able to extricate myself from her clutches only after she had scratched my neck and back. I fled into the building, crying out and running up the stairs in that kind of nightmare frenzy in which the legs do not work and the steps never end. Jill's mother followed in hot, overweight pursuit. I was screaming for my life, and she was screaming in pursuit of that life.

My youth and speed got me to the door of our apartment, but only seconds ahead of her. Frantically I rang the bell and waited in agonized frustration for my mother to notice the blinking lights, tripped by a special mechanism that would alert her. I could hear her slowly approaching the door while Jill's mother thundered up the stairs behind me. My mother could not, of course, hear my hysterical screams. The door opened miraculously just as Jill's mother reached the landing and was about to tear me to pieces. I slipped around my mother and ran into the bedroom, where I hid behind the door. Some limited interchange followed in which Jill's mother tried to tell my mother what she thought I had done. The door closed without my mother saying anything or defending me.

When my mother came to see me, I was in that phase of sobbing where it is impossible to talk or breathe. When I calmed a bit, I told her what had happened. I think she understood I was not to blame, but she never said anything to Jill's mother. She just bathed the long, deep scratches down my back and on my neck, and told me not to worry. No intercession was possible. My mother could not engage in that kind of complex verbal reprisal. One just suffered in silence, remembering not to cry over spilt milk.

I never spoke to Jill or her mother again.

When I arrived from Paris at Kennedy Airport, that night after my mother was hit by the truck in 1972, I rushed to my brother's apartment. As I walked down the corridor, I could see him and my father waiting for me. Their faces were ravaged with grief, like Greek masks of woe. But I had steeled myself in order to make the flight. I looked aloof, blank. My father and my brother were searching my face for the tears and the grief they had been sharing, for the kinship they now found briefly in mourning. I merely embraced them and said, "Let's go to the hospital."

There we met with the doctor, who told us there was no hope. My mother was brain dead. She had been hit by the truck and had fallen on the asphalt pavement just alongside the curb. It was around suppertime and she had gone, probably in a hungry haze, from the Hebrew Association of the Deaf on 14th Street, to get a sandwich at a diner on Second Avenue. As she crossed the street, the light changed. A truck came around the corner and must have sounded its horn, but what is a honking horn to a deaf person? She saw a car coming, tried to turn back, and was hit by the truck. A woman who was at her side said my mother was unconscious immediately. She felt no pain. At the hospital she was pronounced DOA. The doctors managed to transfuse her and get her heart beating, but her brain had been deprived of oxygen for too long.

My father insisted that there could be a miracle. My brother and I listened to the grim news. Then I said, "I want to see her." My brother said, "It's better to remember her the way she was." Neither he nor my father had gone into her hospital room during the twenty-four hours she had been there. The only thing in life that seemed important to me was to hold her hand, kiss her face, and stay with her—even if she was unconscious. I asked my brother where her room was, and he pointed vaguely through two double doors. He repeated, as did my father, "Better to remember her the way she was."

I went through the doors and looked for her room but could not find it. Since my brother had never been to see her, perhaps he was mistaken? As I walked around in confusion, I began to feel dread rising. I imagined her mutilated body, swollen and crushed beyond recognition by the truck, bloated, purple, attached to machines. My resolve began to subside. *Better to remember her the way she was.* Separation and denial swirled in the hallway, fed in currents by my father and brother, by my family way of life. My mother would have said the same thing: "Better to remember her the way she was."

I turned around, back through the double doors, which swung with a final thud. I never saw her alive again.

We went back to my brother's apartment. I still had not cried. My brother's wife, Monica, opened the convertible sofa in the living room and my father and I prepared to share the bed. He put on his striped pajamas, shuffled around crushed in despair, as I lay embedded in emotional concrete. He turned off the lights and muttered the same prayer he muttered every night of his life, his deaf version of Hebrew, *"Baruch atah adonai elohanu melech hawolum* . . . God bless Mother, Father, Janey, Natalie, Brother Aby, Eva, Gerald, and Lenny," and got into bed. We hugged each other. I began to cry. I reached down into my soul and cried with a depth I have rarely felt. The dark, the night, my father's pathetic prayer all plumbed my complete self. I felt the pain of all the years combine with the pain of the moment. My brother came out of his bedroom, and we all cried together. We needed no words. There was the silence and the gesture. That seemed familiar, and that seemed enough.

The next day the doctor called and said my mother was dead. My father, who had held to a belief that there would be a miracle, collapsed and stopped breathing. I gave him artificial respiration and within minutes we were rushing in an ambulance to the same hospital where my mother had just died. I held my father's hand and signed to him that I loved him, the ASL phrase being so physical, like the hug itself. I realized at that moment that I did love him.

He was released after observation. Then we received a phone call from the coroner saying that, because my mother's death would be considered a homicide, we would have to identify my mother in the morgue. Of course, no one had seen her since the accident. Perhaps it was not she! Perhaps she had wandered off in a daze, a case of amnesia, as did Ronald Coleman in the film *Random Harvest* when he is hit by a car and forgets his former life. Neither my brother nor I wanted to go alone to the morgue. Better to remember her the way she was. But now the law compelled us to see her. We decided to go together—one of the few times in our lives when either of us asked the other for help.

The morgue was near the East River. We took a cab together in silence and fear. We would have to look on the body of our mother, perhaps horribly mutilated. We waited in a dull gray room until a man came out and told us to go down a set of steps and pass by a door. He told us to glance quickly in the door and then continue on. I had an image of the morgue from movies I had seen: bodies on slabs in refrigerated filing cabinets with tags on their toes. Or Zola's view in *Thérèse Raquin* of the naked, bloated bodies on display for prurient inspection of the public, their sex visible.

My brother and I were both afraid. He went first, as the oldest I suppose, and I saw him at the bottom of the stairs. He took one look, broke into tears, and fled down the corridor. I walked slowly down the steps, prepared to look quickly and turn, as I had as a small boy when I saw my mother naked for the first time, stepping out of the shower.

Her body was on a gurney, draped with a sheet so that only her face showed. She looked beautiful. I started to turn, as I had prepared myself to do. Then I stopped and looked back. I gazed slowly and lovingly on her. Someone had gathered her hair and pulled it back in an uncharacteristic way that made her look elegant. One small scratch marred her nose; otherwise there was not a mark on her. In death her nose seemed a bit more prominent, actually noble. She was beautiful in this repose. I could not stop looking.

Finally I walked away. I had missed my chance to sit by her side in her last hours because I had feared her disfigurement. How ironic that I had never learned to transcend the disability of physical trauma. Even now, more than twenty-seven years later, I still feel pangs of regret.

My brother's memory of this moment, unlike mine, was one of horror. He still insists that she was wrapped in black. I see her angelic in white. He wishes he had never gone. I wish I had stayed longer.

Brother's Keeper

And the Lord said, "What have you done? The voice of your brother's blood is crying to me from the ground."

.—Genesis 8:10

My brother, Gerald, was an only child for ten years. Of that era I know very little. There are family stories, and there is the cat-o'-nine-tails that stood in the corner of the closet. It was always a symbol of the past—of the time before me, the era of Hammurabi's Code. Our parents had bought a whip to use on my brother because he had what they and his teachers deemed a behavior problem. In reality, he was hyperactive, aggressive with other children, and generally unsocialized. They did not have these descriptors, so they just called him "bad." They used the whip to exorcise whatever life force he possessed. By the time I was small, the whip was no longer actively used; rather, it was referred to as a potential punishment. Evoking its name usually sufficed to make us behave. I always recalled my brother's stories of having been struck repeatedly.

Emotions did not go down well in our family. Our father alone was grudgingly allowed to express them. We called him "moody," but at least he had moods. We boys were expected to be always alert, clean, dressed, and ready for life—cooperative; not depressed, angry, or truculent. I managed to retain my emotional life by a combination of my own sheer obstinacy and my aging parents' flagging powers. Because my brother bore the full force of their youthful zeal in parenting, surely he suffered the most.

One story my mother told me was of the time when she and my brother's second-grade teacher hatched a plan to scare him into less hyperactive behavior. (This plan would probably be considered child abuse now, but so would the whip.) The teacher called my mother and brother to school and arranged for him to "overhear" her telling Mother that, if he did not improve his behavior, he was going to be sent to reform school. Of course, this was all a show put on to terrify my brother, and I believe it succeeded. Between the whip and the scare tactics, he began to behave. And that repression only worsened his problems by causing him to dissociate from his feelings. He became robotic, a sleepwalker through emotional life. He was a terrified child who had no friends. Another teacher actually contacted my mother to arrange a play date for him when he was ten years old.

When I look at early photographs of my brother, I see an ovoid head with buck teeth. These were taken before my time. My personal memory of him begins with his teenage years and braces. A photograph shows the two of us against the yellowish brick wall and treeless street of our apartment building. By now a sullen adolescent, he faces the box camera. In the background, my head virtually shaved, I ride my bike, trying to have a good time despite the joyless mood. The picture captures my essential childhood; seeking out joy amidst barrenness and depression. I ride on, my creaky tricycle whirling up what little enjoyment there is to be spun out of this life.

Like most adolescents, Gerald spent much of his time combing his hair, staring at himself in the mirror, and otherwise asserting his proto-adult self. I was his perfect observer and object, the one who gazed at him gazing at himself. The one he would always be stronger than, bigger than, able physically and mentally to coerce and compel. I admired him. He was already the young man I hoped to become.

I remember watching him bathe. He would lie in the water; I would sit on the closed lid of the toilet, observing. It was a mutual occasion for exhibitionism and the gaze. His body was newly touched with the attributes of manhood. I would look at his pubic hair, his genitals, and the small curl of hair over his sternum. He would vigorously soap his penis. I still remember the squishy sound of soap against skin. We would clearly worship his newly wrought body together, like Adam looking in wonder at the creation of flesh. His physique was so different from my own smooth, pale, pudgy form, which lacked the slightest suggestion of musculature.

So much of my relationship to Gerald was in the intersection between the body and language. He would stand in front of the mirror in his shorts and admire himself, saying, "Tower of Power," the phrase used in a television advertisement for Texaco. I would try to add, as fast as I could, the word "gasoline." He would simultaneously try to add the word "muscle." It was as if I could neutralize his body, his narcissism, his power over me, by returning the Tower of Power to Texaco, but he retained both the tower and the power.

He used to sing a song to himself in the mirror:

Gerald J. Julius, Gerry, J. D. Davis,
Better known as the King of the World.

The effect was not meant to be funny or ironic. Rather, it was a will to power, a statement of sovereignty that would proclaim itself from Clinton Avenue to the Bronx to New York to the world at large. My brother had to surround himself with mantras of strength, incantations that would transform the image in the mirror into the world's strongest man. Whether I was for it or against it, I was always a willing observer, a sort of accomplice.

Since Gerald could not do battle with our father, who had so clearly armed himself against the world, he turned his pent-up anger on me.

Powerless in the face of his superior, he exerted authority over his inferior. My life with him was a delicate dance between yearning for his approval and tolerating his sadistic attentions. I admired him so much that I was willing to let him harm me.

The era I remember most distinctly began around my fifth birthday, which would have made my brother at least fifteen. Although it still hard for me to believe that a fifteen-year-old would even bother taking the time to torture a five-year-old, I remember too well many of the horrors he inflicted on me. His approach was based on consistency. Every day he would perform acts of domination. He did this as part of a mirthless, systematic routine. He was not angry with me; he acted not in retribution for a specific "crime" on my part. Rather, he would grimly exact his toll on me as if his job involved practicing the banality of evil. He was a full-time sadist, and I was the human time clock he punched in every day.

First was trial by suffocation. He would lie on me, wrap me up in a blanket, and otherwise smother me. Claustrophobia was my supreme fear, one that they would have known about in Orwell's Room 101. As my ultimate torturer, Gerald capitalized on this knowledge. I would begin to panic, beg to be released, and cry hysterically. He seemed to derive a great deal of satisfaction from compacting me.

Second was trial by Pavlovian conditioning. He would punch me routinely; then he would feint punching me. If I did not flinch, he would punch me again, until I was conditioned to flinch every time he made a swift gesture. All of this was done methodically, with a slight smile of malice, but never any overt anger or cause. He would do this anywhere from once to a dozen times daily.

Third was trial by skilled torture. He knew every pressure point on my body and would routinely squeeze the tendons behind my knees, the top of my kneecap, the space between the tendons on the back of my neck. The pain was like electricity shooting through my body. I could not fight back; I could not do anything to him, since he was so much bigger. My screams of course produced no reaction, since our mother in the other room could not hear me. If I tattled on my brother, either he would take his revenge later or our mother would wearily come in the bedroom and say to him, "Stop starting!" Her catch-all admonition had a certain rhetorical flourish, but it never worked. I do not remember my brother ever being punished. For my part, there was no escape. I simply accepted the torture as part of my life, even as I continued to hope that Gerald would like me.

Fourth was trial by choking. I wrestle with my brother, who mounts me, pins my shoulders to the bed, and then says, "Eat this blanket." The blanket is green and woolly. I remember only too well his shoving it into my mouth, coldly demanding, "Eat it! Eat it!" I was trapped in my claustrophobic nightmare, gagging on soggy wool. I remember swallowing a small bit, in ritual suffering.

Fifth was trial by water. After having been almost drowned at the Crotona Park pool, I was leery of swimming places. My brother rarely accompanied us to Orchard Beach, but when he did, his favorite activity involved taking me out to water over my head and threatening to drown me. Helpless as I was in his arms, I screamed and begged to be brought back to the shore. He laughed. When we got back to shore, he would call me a baby and say I was afraid of the water. Indeed I was, at perhaps four years old.

My own children much later invented a beach game that involves carrying their parents "like babies" in the ocean. As I was held in my son's arms, in the warm waters of the Mediterranean, I suddenly remembered the terror of being held in my brother's arms in the cold surf off the Bronx. Adult now, I was able dimly to understand what a life lesson it would have been to feel secure in my brother's arms, rather than discovering at such an early age that I should trust no one.

Sixth in the list of tortures was trial by automobile. My brother would sometimes (rarely) be assigned to take me outside and watch me. On such occasions, out of the gaze of our parents, he had full rein to do as he wished. He would pull me out in the middle of the street and hold me in the path of a looming though beautifully air-streamed De Soto or

Pontiac until the very last moment, when he would release me so I could scramble to the curb in a frenzy of grief and relief as the car rumbled by. Seventh was trial by mental anguish. He would pretend that he was not my brother but only a robot named Mr. X. Whenever I called him Gerald, he would say he was Mr. X. Whenever I called Him "Mr. X," he would say he was Gerald and that Mr. X had gone on his steed Pegasus to Vas Legas, where he apparently lived while not engaged in duping me. I searched the house for the sliding panel behind which Mr. X was kept when he was not in Vas Legas. I really believed it was behind the mirror in the living room, if only I could figure out what panel to push or pull. This ruse was the most painful of all to me. I rarely connected with my brother; he was so often a robot. An apt metaphor for his rather detached sadism.

One day the Mr. X gambit became too much to bear. I abandoned my policy of long-standing suffering and threw a tornado of a tantrum. My display of emotion was so disturbing that he begged me not to let our parents know. He ran off to Dollinger's toy store to buy me a toy as a bribe that would insure my silence. But though our mother could not hear my cries, she saw my florid, tear-stained face, and I finally told her all about Mr. X. When Gerald returned bearing the toy, he saw that the jig was up. I realized for the first time that my emotions could defeat my brother's physical strength, and that I could tell our parents something which might affect my fate.

Since both of our parents were connected by their deafness, I longed for connection with my brother. He seemed to know the world of the hearing, although now I see that much of that attitude was a bluff designed to fool himself and anyone else. I was willing to tolerate almost any kind of behavior toward me, even to excuse it. Only later did I realize how angry, hurt, and disappointed I was with the fact that he was unable to help me enjoy the fullness of life with him. He might have been a caring, helping presence. We might have sought each other for solace and comfort. But he could not pull himself up out of his well of anger and pain, at least some of which had arisen from the fact that my birth ended his decade of solo attention from our parents. And he himself was the victim of our father's control and temper. The strange part is that my brother rarely expressed verbal anger toward me. He just poked, prodded, pinched, punched, squeezed, and noogied me into sullen compliance.

I never really resisted my brother because I realized that a decade's age difference made me too weak to match his adolescent size and strength. Crying did me no good, since our parents couldn't hear and Gerald was careful to bother me when no one else could see. In addition, I so desperately wanted his approval that I colluded in his games of abuse.

When I was about seven and he seventeen, there was a decisive emotional moment between us. It was Yom Kippur, the holiest day of the Jewish year. Following the Orthodox laws, no electric lights were illuminated, no radio or television turned on. My family sat together and talked in the candle-lit kitchen. Then my brother and I went into the bedroom. In the twilight we began to wrestle on the beds, action that often served as a prelude to my being hurt. Suddenly I pushed my brother with my feet. He fell off the bed and crashed his head against the metal edge of the frame. He actually began to cry in pain. A strange air of cognitive dissonance hung over the scene: it was my brother who was hurt and crying, not me. He said through his tears, "Why did you do that? You really hurt me." I had broken the rules and injured him in a fight. It was always supposed to be the other way around.

My initial feeling was one of tremendous guilt. I also hoped he wasn't angry, since I still wanted him to like me. But later and deeper there emerged a sense of triumph: I had slain the giant. David and Goliath. St. George and the Dragon. Seven with One Blow. Jack the Giant Killer. I can't say that life turned around and my brother never hurt me again, but there was a subtle memory, a memory of danger and revenge. A warning lingered in the air.

I remember walking along with my family at night, strolling in the September air, seeing search lights in the Bronx sky. In the 1950s were there still search lights looking for enemy planes? I somehow connected that wariness on the part of the great United States, still shining lights in the skies to detect a sneak attack, with the new vulnerability of my big brother. He could be hurt. There could be war.

I should not leave the impression that all my early memories of my brother are negative. Because he was hearing and older, he showed me many things that our parents could not. He connected me to the outer world. It was because he needed a telephone when he started to date that we got our first phone. It was because of his interest in rock and roll that we got a radio, and then a phonograph. It was he who opened my eyes to films. When he was in college, he subscribed to the avant-garde *Film Quarterly,* and he went to see foreign films such as *La Dolce Vita,* which played at the only art house in the Bronx. I was too young to be admitted then, but when I was older, I saw all the European films I could at the Museum of Modern Art. Gerald also decided that I should know about sex. After asking our parents, he showed me pictures of sperm and eggs in his zoology textbook. In many ways I followed in his footsteps, becoming a summer camp counselor and then a bellhop in the Catskills. It took me a long time to realize that I was not a carbon copy of Gerald.

Much of what he taught was more applicable to his own situation than to mine. I recall his advice on how to act on dates: "Tell women what to do; they like that in a man." He told me that when I took a date to a movie, I should always tell her to sit in a specific seat. When I was in summer camp, I tried that with Zina Klapper: "Sit here," I commanded. Perhaps this authoritarian approach did not appeal to her, because she refused to let me put my arm around her in the darkness.

Gerald's advice grew increasingly at variance with my generation's values, especially as the 1960s progressed. His goal was to become the man in the gray flannel suit. His politics were conservative, and his beliefs were those of a slightly earlier age cohort than my own.

Many of our better times together occurred after my brother started attending college. Although he lived at home while a City College student, he no longer seemed to need to hurt me physically. I was no doubt an annoying presence, wanting to play with him as he sat at the card table in the living room and tried to study. Ironically, instead of being the focus of his attention, as I had been in earlier years, now I was someone to be ignored. I hovered like a gnat, my irritating buzz attempting to distract him from his schoolwork, his radio, his life outside the home.

At the end of his sophomore year Gerald was in a state of confusion. Although our parents wanted him to become a physician, he decided to transfer to business school, realizing that tending to people's physical (let alone emotional) needs would not be his forte. He wanted to make money, attain status, and live the good life. But he also wanted to be creative. He decided to work in summer-stock theater. Our parents refused to let him go. Mother, in a rare moment of anger, called him "a drifter." This was one of the very few instances when I can recall seeing my brother upset. Such moments of crisis in his life have paradoxically been precious to me (I have witnessed perhaps four of them), for it is as if the Great Wall of defense buckles for a moment, never longer than a day or two, and my brother becomes a person who shows real emotions. This is the same brother who has often told me, without irony, that he has never experienced guilt and rarely felt anger, shame, or depression.

At that time, when I was about ten and he twenty, I remember having one of those special conversations in which I felt that I could help him because he was willing to reveal his true feelings. He tearfully related his frustrations with Mom and Dad. I felt privileged merely to listen. He was hurt by Mother's condemnation, all the more so because she normally supported us against our father.

After a brief struggle, he finally acquiesced. He did not go to summer stock.

After college Gerald went on a long trip to Europe. When he returned, he entered the army. After his service he decided to take the creative road, to become a film director. Our parents were horrified that he would forsake potential security, instead devoting himself to the famously fickle arts. They viewed life in workers' terms: get a steady job, pay the bills, don't rock the boat. His actions seemed defiant beyond words—defiant not only of his elders but of Fate itself.

He obtained a job as a film editor, but instead of preparing montages on Fellini-like films, he subtitled English films into Spanish for distribution in Latin America. Within a few months he joined an advertising agency and from then on stayed within the business sphere, working subsequently in import-export and eventually entering the world of insurance and investment.

Our relations now are cordial, as they have been for most of our adult lives. We speak on the telephone once a week. He is always "fine"—a coping phrase we learned from our father, whose dying assertion was that he was "fine." Our phone calls are predictable, reporting on our jobs, our children and families, what movies we have seen.

Recently our relationship has grown more intimate. Not over emotions so much, but over writing. Gerald has been writing novels surreptitiously for the past twenty years, jotting them down on the commuter train from Westport to New York each morning. They feature a hard-boiled detective who talks tough and attracts women like honey does bees. I had been working on a different kind of literary and academic novel. Each of us was wary about showing our work to the other, but we took the risk and each ended up admiring what the other had written, finding points of contact that perhaps surprised us.

Our parents' courtship correspondence of the 1930s also helped to unite Gerald and me in the 1990s. As I began to edit *Shall I Say a Kiss?: Courtship Letters of a Deaf Couple* for publication by Gallaudet Press, my brother wanted to become involved in the process. At my suggestion he wrote the volume's preface. Working on the volume brought us closer to our parents and to each other.

While I can honestly conclude this chapter on a positive note, I cannot minimize or dismiss the conflicts described in the preceding pages. I found it particularly difficult to write this chapter because, unlike our parents, my brother is still alive and well. He asked me repeatedly if he could read this memoir-in-progress, and I always replied that he could see it only in its final form. I harbor misgivings about revealing certain aspects of my life, releasing myself into a world that does not know me. But this painful sibling relationship is so much a part of the dynamic of my life that, if I tell my story, I must tell a part of Gerald's.

I have finally shown him this memoir, and he has read it avidly. I think he has come to understand how odious his behavior was to me, and he sincerely regrets it. His is an apology I can fully accept now, and I am grateful to know that he understands me better, even as I think I have come to understand him.

Honeymoon with Mom

My remembered sexual life began together with my remembered entry to death. And all of that began with my ocean voyage to England when I was just about to turn eight years old. I thought of this trip as my honeymoon, because only my mother and I were going to visit her family in London and Birmingham. My father had to work. My brother was going off to be a counselor in summer camp.

I remember the thrill of anticipation that came with knowing I was leaving my humdrum existence in the Bronx. I, a small boy from Tremont Avenue, was going to walk up the accommodation ladder onto the famous ocean liner the *Queen Elizabeth* and sail over the bounding main for Jolly Old England.

I couldn't sleep the night before we were to go down to the docks. And of course I could only gag over breakfast. Mrs. Zuckerman offered to drive us to the Cunard Line pier. Waiting alone in her car, I smelled the automobileness of the upholstery and reveled in the knobs and dials. I could not believe that I would soon be ocean bound. Jill emerged from the apartment building. I called out her name in excitement, but then—remembering what her mother had done to me—I quickly slid down in the seat; when she turned around, she saw no one. When I returned that fall, she had moved away.

When we arrived at the docks, there was the *Queen Elizabeth,* hulking above us. Its sheer size was astounding. It was beautiful, the culmination of centuries of shipbuilding; especially to a small boy, it might as well have been the Taj Mahal. My father was with us, my brother being off at camp by now. We boarded the ship together, as did hundreds of other seafaring folk and their guests. We walked around, admiring the size and the appointments of the ship. Everything was elegant and gleaming. The main-level bulkheads were paneled with deep mahogany, the floors plush with rich carpeting, the walls festooned with polished brass fixtures. There could not have been a starker contrast than between the *Queen Elizabeth* and our apartment house.

Then a man with a bullhorn circulated through the hundreds who were saying farewell and announced decisively that all visitors had to disembark in twenty minutes. I instantly panicked. My parents could not hear the man, and I feared that my father would accidentally remain on the boat, a stowaway. If he had to come to England with us, he would ruin my honeymoon with my mother.

I signed to him, "Time to get off."

"Plenty of time," he signed back confidently.

"No! Hurry! Rush! Man says, Time to get off."

No encouragement could speed his tedious farewell. After all, this was the man who would stand for half an hour at the front door, with his galoshes and hat still dripping from the rain, telling all about the trivia of his workday. Of course, it didn't occur to me that he probably wanted to savor those last minutes with his wife before their first-ever two-month separation. Or perhaps it occurred too well to me? I threw a tantrum of epic proportions, and my father left the boat to placate me.

My mother and I looked over the side of the ship, from our towering height, trying to find his bald head among the throng of well-wishers. We wanted to wave as the ship was tugged out of the slip, but we could not find him. He was lost to us. And I had prevented him from waving good-bye. My will triumphed, although my guilt nagged me.

Our cabin was a tiny room below the water line. I believe we shared it with another person. Could it have been a man? Would they have allowed that, or is this only a phantom echo of my father's banished presence? I was a terrible sailor who began vomiting almost as soon as the boat left the harbor. My mother was rather proud of her sea legs; she said her whole family were good sailors. Which obviously put me in a different family.

This voyage awoke my sense of class distinctions. I loved to wander the corridors and rooms of this enormous vessel, like a tiny Jonah inside a motorized steel whale. I came upon a door that said "Only Second Class Passengers may enter." I opened it and peeked in, beholding an even richer world of plusher carpets, softer armchairs, and deeper colors. My section suddenly seemed duller, dingier, chintzier, more like the yellow buildings of the Bronx. I wanted to cross this class barrier, to pass through the doors to this other world, but even then I knew I was constitutively not second class, let alone first class. I was a steerage type. A painful feeling of exclusion came over me. Like many victims of oppression, I took the lowly place I was assigned. Shame more powerful than any door prevented me from entering that upper world.

The ocean crossing was still a glorious time of freedom for me. I left my mother and went wherever I wanted, without fear and without permission. The ship harbored no criminals, no marauding youth gangs, no nameless dreads. Perhaps because I could hear and I was now my mother's sole mate, she deferred to me. I told her when various bells sounded for lifeboat drills; I relayed announcements as they were made. I was the fount of information, and she was my minion. I was on my own. No one could trace my origin to a one-bedroom apartment on a dingy street in the Bronx.

I made friends with other children. I played shuffleboard with old men, one of whom renamed me "Skipper"—a suitably nautical moniker that I prized even more than the white skipper's cap that the old man let me wear occasionally. Each day a printed calendar of events was slipped under our door. I remember best the movie screenings, and two films in particular stay in my mind: *The Delicate Delinquent,* with Jerry Lewis, and *The Woman in a Dressing Gown,* with Sylvia Syms. The latter, which I have never seen again, haunted my mother and consequently impressed me. It was about a woman whom today we would call an agoraphobic. She stays home all day in her dressing gown, gets drunk, tries to shape up, dresses and waits for the date who never appears, and so back to the dressing gown. To my mother this film must have represented the desire to stay home forever, a deaf woman without help.

There were transcendent moments on board. The sunsets were glorious, with no land to obscure the horizon. I spent hours hanging over the front railing, watching the monumental spume of water cloven by this awesome ship's gigantic prow. And yet, massive as the *Queen Elizabeth* was, it often tossed like a teacup. When the seas got rough, I alone would remain on deck. Whereas others would retire to the coziness of the dining room, I could not go below, lest I become more violently ill. My mother would ask the steward to pack me a lunch, and she would bring it as I sat in the only lounge chair not lashed to the deck. At these times I watched the horizon rise above the boat, like a giant *tsunami,* and then fall out of sight. The skies were dark and sinister, and I would sit under some metallic overhang like a seven-year-old valetudinarian soon to die. My mother finally lost patience and told me she could not bring another sandwich. I glumly arose on my rickety legs and proceeded, gorge rising, to the nicely appointed dining room. The waiter brought my soup bowl. Anticipating his pouring of soup by several nano-seconds, I vomited neatly into the bowl. This act of perfect timing caught our tablemates unaware, perhaps even stunned them by the incredible neatness of the disgusting event. After that, my mother let me return to solitude on the deck.

We arrived first at Cherbourg, then made our landing at Southampton. We were met by relatives new to me. My aunt Betty, who had actually carried me home from the hospital when I was born, and her husband Bernard, cradling their baby daughter Michelle, took us to their flat at The Angel in London. I remember loving the names, admiring that a neighborhood should be called "The Angel" rather than "East Tremont Avenue." They lived modestly and ate horrible British food. (All my relatives seemed to have a penchant for piling baked beans on top of everything, including even fried eggs.)

At my Aunt Betty's I saw my cousin Michelle being diapered. That vision of her nudity ignited neural paths never before known. I said nothing, but I took it all in. I watched as Michelle had tantrums in her crib and pounded her head repeatedly against the wall. My mother suggested a night-light candle, and my Aunt Betty, who was an older mother, rushed around nervously, trying to manage things. The candle seemed to help.

Then we stayed with my Uncle Max and his wife, Anne. They lived in one of those little red-brick row houses that are quintessentially English. There I fell in love with my cousin Naomi. I hated it when she lorded her few years over me at bedtime: I had to retire ignominiously to a folding hassock an hour before she went to bed. I used to amuse my relatives by singing patriotic American songs while wearing my "God Bless America" tie. Everyone said what a nice boy I was, and what a good job my mother had done in raising me, even though she was deaf.

Uncle Max sat in his armchair. Aunt Anne cooked. She always said, "Not to worry," so everyone did. I can't remember any aspect of life there except sitting in the living room, listening to the Kingston Trio, and eating bad food. I recall going to Covent Garden and to an opera, but I had no idea what was happening. Music to me was so alien that the experience was like watching a somewhat tedious and annoying visual display with interminable discordant notes.

I remember being taken to Greenwich to see the Prime Meridian. My cousin Lez took his sister Naomi and me on the boat ride down the

Thames. There before me was a long strip sunk into the ground. I jumped on it and leaped back and forth across it, as children do with abstract markers. I was told that this was the place where time began. Unsure exactly what that meant, I sensed that if I stood on the line, I would somehow be at the center of time, at the beginning of the world. Everything else would emanate from here, the center of civilization. I took this personally and thought with awe, "I am at the center of time. All things start here with me." Childhood narcissism is the best and purest kind.

We went to Birmingham to visit Aunt Celia and Uncle Jack, their son Harold, and my mother's father, Eli Weintrobe, who lived with them. I remember this stay with a wonderful fog of pleasure. We were in a house with real people who seemed alive and had the quality of not being deaf. Harold was the older brother I never had. He was engaged to be married to a Scottish-Jewish X-ray technician named Benita. He would take me to her work, and she would X-ray various parts of my body for fun. (Somewhere I still have the X-ray of my little arm with cuff link visible.) He would play with me, joke with me, and never once did he make me eat a blanket or shove me in front of an oncoming car. I didn't know quite what to do with such largesse of good feeling.

Uncle Jack was one of those men whose skinniness is directly attributable to cigarette smoking. His face was a twisted set of cables surrounding a cigarette. But he was a warm-hearted man, a bit of a wag, whose great pleasure was teasing everyone—best of all, me. He would say to Aunt Celia that my mother was the prettiest of the three sisters: "Eva's the best of the lot." He owned a dry-cleaning store, and I would go there every day with him. Three or four women worked in the back, and they all called me "Luv." Teatime seemed to occur with incredible frequency; I would join in drinking the dark, alien beverage. The brew tasted awful, as I picked out the bits of leaves from my teeth, but I liked the adultness of drinking it. Pinups of semi-clad beauties decorated the drab back room. (I never understood why women would work surrounded with these pictures.) Consequently, the shop seemed sexual to me. Seamy but amusing, alien, and erotic.

If there were signs of my sexual awakening, there were also ill omens. Two memories of my English days stay with me. In one I am learning to ride a bicycle. Naomi is holding the back of bicycle as I go down a long hill. I tell her to slow down. I am going too fast. Then I look around and see her, a distant figure halfway up the hill. She has let me go on my own. I turn forward again and behold the world careening toward me. Suddenly a huge tree trunk looms up, and I crash into it. The second memory is of sitting in Uncle Jack's green mini-station wagon. He has gone into the house to get something, and I leap into the driver's seat to play. Delighted at the novelty of being behind the wheel, I play for a second, only to realize that the car is beginning to move slowly forward down the hill. It picks up speed as I panic. Just then Uncle Jack jumps in and stops the car. This is virtually the first time I have been saved by someone since the unknown bather pulled me out of the Crotona Park swimming pool. I am again amazed that I can be saved by someone other than my small self, but I am also aware of how quickly the safe becomes unsafe.

I remember music in all these houses, music in every house but my own. We went to see *Around the World in Eighty Days,* and the simple fact that my cousin Harold and I could sing the music together felt like a triumph of the human will. The coziest moments I can recall are sitting in the armchair with Uncle Jack, eating Rollos, slurping on the caramel interiors that slowly became revealed after the chocolate melts in minute degrees, and watching the best (which is to say the worst) of British television. Here was more domesticity, indulgence, comfort, security, and happiness than I had ever known. I could enjoy the television without having to explain everything to my Uncle Jack: he could hear!

My grandfather, Eli, lived in this house. My childhood was characterized by an absence of grandparents. My mother's mother died before I was born. In my bedroom hung a picture of her squinting into the sun. My mother told me that she had a very painful disease in which her eyelashes grew into her eyes. I couldn't tell if the squinting was the sun or the eyelashes. My father's mother had died when I was very young. My grandfather Solomon lived in California; I saw him only a few times before he also died. So Eli Weintrobe was basically my only living grandparent. Despite this unique tie, I was afraid of him. I felt guilty for harboring that fear, but when I saw him he looked like an old, bald, palsied ghost with strangely large ears and small, bloody eyes sunk down into huge, soulful sockets. He smelled like old linens and stale lemons. He seemed to live in some uncertain place in the house that I never saw, and he rarely came down from wherever that was. When he did appear, his hands shook terribly; he spoke in a thick Yiddish accent. Try as I might, I felt no affection for him. I do not even remember my mother, his daughter, kissing him or cuddling up to him. Perhaps she was afraid of him, too. I do not know what he felt for me as he touched me with his marmoreal hands. Strange notes written in Yiddish were left in the outhouse, a relic from an earlier time, since now the family had indoor plumbing. Eli seemed to like the outhouse, a reminder of his youth in Poland, perhaps. He seemed like a man from faraway places and times, not the grandfather I needed.

One day he came down from on high and asked me to go to Shabbos service with him. I suppose he wanted to show off his grandchild from America. I was afraid: I did not want to go to a strange synagogue in a foreign country with him. But he really wanted me to accompany him, and he offered me money. To my shame, I accepted. Like a small Judas, I clutched my pieces of silver and proceeded in bad faith past the brick row houses to the decrepit synagogue. The place had the fallen splendor common to many *shuls*. All the old men were there, muttering and praying. I remember the awkwardness of everything. My proud grandfather introduced me to a retinue of palsied men who patted my head with quavering hands.

I sat in the pew feeling depressed and aware that even the songs had different tunes than those I had heard at the Young Israel of Tremont. My grandfather leaned over and whispered in my ear that I should watch carefully: I would see the bride of Shabbos enter. This was news to me. I had not known about the bride of Shabbos. My grandfather told me that the Sabbath would appear as a beautiful young woman dressed for a wedding. I watched and even hoped that this gray and maudlin place, this droning, morose service, would be magically transformed. My imagination met my desire. Suddenly the bride did appear, shyly entering, festooned in flowers and exuding a perfumed aura. I did think I could see her come into the synagogue. She was lovely. She looked like my cousin Naomi, with long light brown hair that caught the luster of the Shabbos candles. I let myself relax, there with the figure of death that my grandfather resembled, and I felt the bride of Shabbos upon me. She approached and enfolded me in her arms; I rested my head on her breast, somewhat embarrassed about what the old men, and especially my grandfather, would think. But they nodded and smiled, seeming almost to encourage me. The bride sang along with the oriental, lugubrious tunes, while she let me nestle on her bosom. I was almost lulled to sleep. Then she parted the brocade of her dress and brought out her breast, shining with an almost lunar intensity. My lips could not resist. I took her nipple in my mouth, sucking first slowly, then hungrily, tensing and releasing, holding on for a moment with my teeth, until little pools of milk appeared at the corners of my mouth. The old men were still smiling. My grandfather put his hand on her breast and stroked gently. I knew now why he had wanted me to come to the synagogue. This was his secret retreat, an oasis for comfort, before he climbed the stairs to his remote room. This was the family secret he passed on to me: in times of need I could call on this presence for comfort, for solace, through the dark ages and death that surrounded me.

A year later my grandfather was dead. I answered the telephone call from England. I could not keep from smiling that nervous smile with which children greet the news of death. My mother collapsed in tears as I conveyed the message. I hung up the telephone. My job was done, but what a strange reversal of roles.

My memories of my mother are dim during this time in England. She must have merged back into her family, being there with her sisters and her father whom she had not seen for so long. I do remember sleeping in a double bed with my mother upstairs in some faraway bedroom. This too was a magic secret of my trip to England: I got to sleep with my mother. After all my night terrors of death, after all my early separations by the barrier of silence, I was finally united with my mother at night when I needed her the most. I could reach across the silence now and touch her, call her with my fingers. (Perhaps she was the bride of Shabbos?) After a few nights of sleeping together, she put a pillow between us. She said I moved around too much. I was hurt by that. Why did my mother need to separate herself from me? Was there something else? Was this arrangement too suggestive or improper to her? Did she pick up on my own new claims to her? Did she recognize in me something that I could not even perceive in myself?

We went to visit Stratford-upon-Avon, Shakespeare's birthplace. I stared at the little cradle and the writing table. I saw Anne Hathaway's cottage. I did not really know who Shakespeare was; my mother clearly had very little idea either, other than that he was a famous person. At seven, and in my family, I had a better idea of who Li'l Abner was. I do remember falling into the Avon while trying to pet a swan, to the hilarious laughter of my relatives.

Upon our departure from England a disturbing event unconsciously crystallized my feelings about my relationship to my deaf parents. Aunt Betty and her family took us down to Southampton to the *Queen Elizabeth.* My mother was bringing back some jewelry and cutlery that she did not want to declare at customs. In order to smuggle the goods, she concealed them on me. I had cutlery up my arms and jewelry in my pockets. My mother inadvertently turned me into a criminal by this simple act of concealment. I had to interpret for her when the customs agent asked her if she had anything to declare. I had to say no. I had to tell her that smuggling such items was a crime punishable by imprisonment and a fine. I had to tell him that she understood. Meanwhile the objects under my clothing jingled imperceptibly, but like thunderbolts to my ears. My mother was calm. Although I was humiliated and terrified, I had to maintain my lying exterior to the hostile world. I was not allowed to complain about such activities. I never even realized how upset I was, how unconscionable it was to do something like this to a child, until much later.

After a particularly rough ocean voyage we returned to the Bronx. When we walked into our apartment, everything looked small and dingy, but suspended from the chinning bar under the doorway to the living room were letters that my brother and father had cut out from the magazine section of the *Daily News* to spell "Welcome Home!" Such a display of good feeling was rare and really caught me by surprise. I was delighted, and still am, that one or both of these men thought to go an extra step to welcome us. Of course, we had been gone for more than two months, but in our family we never celebrated much. Birthdays were marked with a quick, off-key rendition of "Happy Birthday to You," a frugal slice of "napoleon" (as my mother called "neapolitan") ice cream, and the smallest cake from the bakery on Tremont Avenue. A few dollars would be put next to the celebrant's plate. On my father's birthday, my mother typically gave my father an envelope with five dollars in it: two weeks later, on her birthday, my father would give the five dollars back. They completely lacked all sense of an occasion. So how amazing and poignant it was to see those letters spelling out their idea of welcome.

Schooling

> "The record of a boy's education interests few save his parents."
>
> —Rudyard Kipling, *Kim*

School was where I was most at home. Paradoxically, my home was like a waiting room, where I sat bored and slightly anxious over what was to come. My parents taught me survival skills. My father taught me to defy expectations by persevering. Race-walking was, for him, a way of excelling in a world that, at that time, did not allow deaf people to excel. My mother, on the other hand, taught me to lie low. She was an expert at simple existence: if she had to make a pot roast, she would make a pot roast. She existed purely in her moment.

But my parents could not teach me about the world, about nature, about ideas. By the time I was born, they were old and tired, possessing just enough energy to perform the necessary functions of life. When my father was not racing or working, he spent most of his time slumped over the *Daily News,* asleep on the couch, or watching baseball. When I was older, I took a photo of him on the couch, newspaper on his lap, head thrown back, mouth open in a snore. I looked up an apt phrase in *Roget's*

Thesaurus and inscribed the picture: "'Thou knowest him well, the god of Sleep' . . . Chaucer."

My mother was a dervish of cooking, cleaning, or sewing. She taught me to thread a sewing machine, and I could darn my socks and sew on buttons. My father was not particularly handy; I think he taught me how to change a light bulb and repair a broken lamp. (Or maybe I taught him.) Luckily, we lived in an apartment building, so the superintendent would come up and repair the dripping faucets, accepting the shot of whiskey my parents offered as a tip.

My brother had learned many things at school, and if he was home and interested, he would teach me. But most of the time he was either out on dates or hunched over a card table in the living room doing his homework, and I had to be quiet so as not to disturb him. If I talked to him at dinner when the radio was on, he would say, "I'm not paying to hear you."

By contrast, school was a magical place of knowledge and discovery. It was a place where adults were interested in me and where my talents were recognized. There was the pleasure of discovery at school. I was initially amazed by the many occasions for celebration because, in my family, changes and occasions were met with a matter-of-fact acceptance. At school we celebrated Arbor Day just to say hello to the trees in spring. We made cut-out turkeys for Thanksgiving. These ordinary acknowledgments of the seasons seemed to me extraordinary festivals.

Schooling began ominously, though. When I was four years old, my mother took me to a nursery school. On the street in front of the school, two dogs were joined, looking quite blasé after mating, and an angry man was yelling at them and pouring hot water on their backs. Whether those two dogs were actually there on my walk, I am not sure, but I remember them in conjunction with nursery school: sexual Cerberuses guarding the way to a loss of innocence. When we went in, I saw children playing in a desultory way. The room was not particularly welcoming. My discomfort was accentuated by some fear that a hypodermic needle was part of the entrance rituals, and I had no intention of being subjected to that rite of passage. In my mind, my mother was part of a conspiracy to poke things into me, and I was a fierce defender of my person. My mother was also adept at not telling me the implications of things, hoping that silence would pave the way for acceptance. She was fond of the enema and the rectal thermometer, a devotee of suppositories, nose drops, and gentian violet painted on the back of an unwilling throat. And she was always there giving tacit approval as doctors injected serum into my buttocks, despite my evasive maneuvers.

My mother asked a few things about the school. Since I was interpreting for her, when the teacher said, "Yes, there was a requirement to be inoculated," I began to scream. My mother, unable to deal with the tantrum, took me out (past the fornicating dogs?) and never brought me back. I learned a lesson about my strength and her passivity.

Instead I went to a summer school that did not require any shots. It was a nice place to glue paper, so a lot of children glued a lot of paper. It lasted for a relatively short time and was only one block from our apartment building, so the anxiety of separation was lessened.

That same summer my mother and I went to camp. It was a camp for the underprivileged of the Bronx, appropriately named Bronx House. I attended every summer, as a camper and then as a counselor, until I was in college. That first summer we were assigned to the "mother and children's camp," a simple collection of cabins on a small lake. The smell of the grass and the woodsy dampness of the cabins filled me with a sense of wonder. It seemed so miraculously different from concrete and asphalt. Up to that point I knew best the streets, the alleyways, and the apartments. But here, in the country, each morning began with all of us singing under a big tree and then eating communally in a large, screened-in recreation hall. Afterwards I was dropped at a small garage where all the youngest children went. There were toys and what I liked best: the little kitchen. The scent of graham crackers and apple juice permeated the place, along with the ever popular poster paint and glue.

My love for the little kitchen indicated an early interest in food. Food was always a symbol of love, of satisfaction—perhaps a way of feeding myself when I was not being fed, metaphorically or otherwise, by my mother. To continue the process of feeding myself, I developed a habit of sneaking off to my cabin room to steal food from my mother's drawer. I said I was going to the bathroom, but instead I headed directly to our room, where we kept a bag of marshmallows. I stuffed myself and returned to the little garage to cook imaginary foods, all the while savoring the powdered marshmallow dust still clinging to my lips. Eventually I was caught (I'm not sure by whom) and suitably humiliated.

As I went off to cut and paste, my mother disappeared from my sight, later returning with handicrafts. She made a little duck of yellow felt. It was the only cuddly thing she ever made for me, and it was my sole stuffed animal. (My parents obviously felt I could get by with the minimum of support. I was helping my parents through the world: What Virgilean guide needs to tote a stuffed animal around in his competent arms?) I went everywhere with my beloved duck. One day I accidentally dropped it into an excavation pit. It came out muddy, and my mother said it was too dirty to keep. I lamented its absence, but she never made me another.

I entered school in the fall. At school I learned to draw, read, and write, all of which I did well. Immediately school became a home for me. (A professor now, I have never left it.) But my entrance to school was accompanied by a great act of repression. I had been a devoted thumb-sucker. Rather than understanding my need for self-comforting, my parents (like so many parents of their generation) saw thumb-sucking as a vice roughly equivalent to heroin addiction. There was also the curse of buck teeth: "If you suck your thumb, get buck teeth. Look at Gerald," my mother would sign, forgetting that her own name sign had a similar toothy reference. My brother had cost my parents much money for orthodontia, so they wanted to avoid the same expense with me. My mother ridiculed me during the day, and at night she painted my thumb with bitter-tasting quinine. Then she bought a small metal cage (devised by the people who brought us the chastity belt?) that fit over my thumb and locked at the wrist. I foiled all attempts to discourage me by simply sucking the cage or switching to my other thumb. My mother finally succeeded where physical barriers had failed by saying, "When you go kindergarten, other children will laugh at you. Think you baby." This threat of humiliation worked magic. The week before I went to kindergarten, I stopped sucking my thumb.

My kindergarten teacher was Mrs. Giordano, a gray-haired lady whose blandness inspired good behavior. I remember spending mornings drawing elaborate warships that bristled with weapons and had glass bottoms that allowed the crew to see under the ocean. I always liked armored machines with lots of defenses and the need for constant surveillance. (Rather like myself?) Mrs. Giordano taught us many self-evident things. I remember getting ready to finger paint. We had what seemed like hours of instruction about how to place the paper, how to use our fingers. Most of all I remember spending days preparing for painting. We practiced with water and brushes at the blackboard until the much-anticipated moment when the real paper and paints were finally brought out. For music, we had sticks and triangles that we banged in proper rhythm as we marched in circles to the regular bass line of Mrs. Giordano's piano accompaniment.

Victor Morabito and Allen Feldman, friends from my apartment building, were in my class, so I felt even more at home. Despite (or perhaps because of) Mrs. Giordano's condescension, I loved school. With Victor at my side constructing equally elaborate warships, and Allen consuming large quantities of Red Hots, we existed in a world separated from our parents. Here I wasn't the son of the deaf people. I was just me.

Or so I thought. Mr. Sidney Nathan Levy, the school principal, took an early interest in me. I am not sure whether it was because of my family background or just because he liked me. In any case, he became the kind of father I wanted: a jovial man with a conspiratorial smile and a pleasant moustache. We had an agreement that when he saw me in the hallways, we would secretly acknowledge each other without making the other children feel bad. Our special signal was to rapidly raise and lower the right-hand pinky. Somehow this "deaf sign" signal seemed more than appropriate, and whenever he appeared, we always waved our digital semaphores. When I was older, Mr. Levy would call me to his office and give me discarded science books, since he knew I was very interested in nature, and we would talk about life and school. It was a wonderful relationship, a slight encouragement that meant the world to me. Once a friend of his came to the school, a scientist, and Mr. Levy arranged a meeting in the library. We talked about telescopes and how much I wanted one. I was desperate to see the stars I had read about in the books Mr. Levy had given me. A few weeks later, two lenses arrived in the mail at home, along with instructions for fabricating a telescope out of the cardboard tubes from a toilet paper roll and a paper towel roll. This frail instrument was a rare treasure for me. I spent hours spying on people and trying to discern the stars and planets that refused to venture forth from the haze of the urban sky. Years later, when I was admitted to Columbia University, I found Mr. Levy's phone number in Yonkers and called to tell him how responsible he was for my academic achievement. That he remembered me was a great comfort.

My first-grade teacher was Mrs. Gory, a large woman with a strange perm that made her look like a giant rag-doll. I recall writing, "Today is Monday. It is sunny and cold." We used the Dick and Jane primer, and I began reading about suburban families with dogs named Spot that ran on lawns. This must have been strange to all of us, who instead played on sidewalks where we saw dogs stuck together.

The real pleasure of first grade involved kissing girls in the clothing closet. Word got out that I liked to do this. Various girls would take my hand and escort me to the closet. Chaste kisses were exchanged, a transcendent experience among overcoats. I fell in love with Anita Berger, a dark-skinned blonde girl who wore a red bandana around her thin neck. She remained my heartthrob throughout grade school. Love among the young is so painful because there is nothing to be done: hand-holding is prohibited by peer pressure; sex is remote and dirty; talking is difficult. So all that remains is longing. I longed without any notion of relief. It wasn't that Anita rejected me—I think she liked me. But there was nothing for her to do.

Two humiliating events occurred when I was in Mrs. Gory's class. The boys' toilet had no doors on the stalls. This lack of privacy was compounded by Mrs. Gory's prerogative to patrol the bathrooms, yelling, "Come on boys, hurry up! Get out of there, will you?" She would march up and down the length of the bathroom while small boys squatted with pants around ankles. I resolved never to be one of those boys. Add to this resolve a chronic state of constipation brought on by my mother's daily fare of ultra-boiled English-Jewish cuisine. One day, as I was writing "Today is sunny and cool," an overwhelming urge of nature came over me. Knowing that the toilet was out of the question, I raised myself slightly from the seat and emitted a small, hard turd the size and shape of a golf ball. Since my pants and underpants were of the baggy, weakened-elastic variety, I let the excremental golf ball roll down my leg and onto the floor. Mrs. Gory was patrolling the classroom, making sure we were not tampering with the poetry of her daily weather report. I looked at the incriminating evidence on the floor under my desk, sized up her position relative to mine, and kicked the offending turd through the legs of my classmates over to the other side of the room. Before long Mrs. Gory happened upon the tell-tale evidence and called out, "Who did this . . . thing?" I said not a word. Shortly the cleaning lady appeared with sawdust and Pine-Sol. I never told and was never found out, but I learned something about secrets and transgression. Unlike the hissing fire that leapt out of the Emerson console in revenge for my transgressions, no hellfire or damnation flashed at me from Mrs. Gory's bleary eyes. No avenging God struck me for fulfilling my father's expectation of uncleanliness. Rather, I had escaped. I had eluded detection, and I learned a powerful lesson about hiding my dark side.

The second humiliating event was Parents' Day. My mother decided to come. (Perhaps I had asked her?) She sat in the classroom, neatly dressed, as usual. She smiled benignly as the class went on, and of course had not a clue about what was being said. During this token visit, which was never repeated, my mother exchanged some pleasantries with my teacher as I interpreted. Mr. Levy came in and told me to tell my mother that I should get a haircut or else play the violin. He acted out the image of someone playing the violin. Neither my mother nor I understood what this meant; violins were not part of our lives, nor were long-haired virtuosi. After that I never told my parents anything about school. It was understood that this was my own world. My parents only saw me at school on two other occasions, for graduations from high school and from college. Both events embarrassed me, but perhaps no more than the average adolescent's humiliation for having parents.

I began to read in Mrs. Gory's class. I remember the day the textbooks were passed out, their covers emitting that oily smell of new books. I flipped through the pages and saw the colorful pictures of suburban families playing on the lawn. I beheld the crispness of the mother's clothing and eyed the rich wool of the father's pants as he smoked his pipe, proudly watching from the doorway. I wanted to read about this world. Even the halting, repeated phrases about balls, dogs, boys, and girls were enough for me. Though my intelligence was insulted and my own home life unrepresented in these volumes, they set me on the path toward reading.

I feel like I learned to read overnight, but in reality at least two years must have passed. I went from these primers to all the books we had at home—not as much of a leap as it seems, for these were confined to one small bookcase in the foyer. We owned a few children's books: *Lad: A Dog,* by Albert Payson Terhune, and *Hello the Boat,* about a family that lived on a houseboat. There was a book of Bible tales for children, and a political satire written by a distant cousin. Supposedly funny, it was unintelligible to me. But I was impressed that someone in my extended family had written a book, and it seemed like a somewhat sacred work, although his name (Anton Gud) made him seem like he could not possibly be part of my family. The remaining books reflected my brother's interest—various sexually explicit novels including *Lady Chatterly's Lover,* Zola's *Nana,* Henry Miller's *Tropic of Cancer,* and Edmund Wilson's *Memoirs of Hecate County.* Another work, *Pornography and the Law,* collected the dirty parts of many different books and used them as text for some unimportant discussions of censorship. What I (and, I assume, most readers) read were the excerpts, not the legal discussions. As soon as I could read well, I plowed through these books again and again. They offered me a world so different from my own, where men and women took deep pleasure in each other—at least as described by the men. I became sexually aroused reading these books, amazed that words could make flesh a reality. I could turn the drab, dull apartment I shared with my deaf parents into a pulsating den of pleasure. I could change the Bronx into the forests of England, where elegant women entered workingmen's cottages and were shaken with mysterious delight. This was a strange revelation, but one that had consequences.

Another book on those shelves, *Facts of Love and Life for Teenagers,* had a contradictory message. The cover showed a big-chested teenage girl wearing one of those tight cashmere sweaters of the period. She glares over her shoulder at a couple who are arm in arm. The text contained much discussion of frogs, rabbits, and at last humans. The section on masturbation said it was OK if not done too often. Such delphic advice was not much help, and the whole book confused me. I returned to *Lady Chatterly's Lover,* somehow knowing that D. H. Lawrence would not have been so ambiguous.

These early encounters with literature confirmed in me a deep and abiding sense that life as depicted in novels was greater than my narrow confines demonstrated. Later, when I began reading Dickens, I instantly grasped that the lives of these poor, deprived characters were like mine, and that my own story was just beginning. Like Oliver, Pip, and David, I would rise from my background and become a gentleman. I would fight injustice and marry a beautiful, erotic woman. I would leave the Bronx and deafness far behind.

At seven I began Hebrew School. My Hebrew School was as if distilled directly from Dickens's brain. It occupied the third floor of a dusty, dingy synagogue on Clinton Avenue. There were only two classrooms, the first taught by Mrs. Hanover, a trim old lady with blue hair, and the older class taught by Mr. Bald, a young rabbi who picked his nose and tapped his knee incessantly. The classrooms bore institutional green paint that had been applied approximately fifty years earlier. Bare lightbulbs glared onto wooden floors that long ago had lost their varnish. The walls were bare. The religious head of the synagogue, Rabbi Paretsky, took our money on the first day and never reappeared.

Mrs. Hanover was very thin and very nervous. She looked like Uriah Heep's mother, and it was into her class I walked that September after I returned from England. There were quiet little Jewish boys and girls sitting in rows, as Mrs. Hanover held her pencil in the air and conducted them in singing some Hebrew song that sounded like Greek to me. I was assigned a seat next to a small blond boy with glasses. His crewcut head seemed to glow like a little electric bulb in the gloom of that place. He smiled shyly and said his name.

Howie Gelman became my lifelong friend. At first I liked him because he was as short as I was. (I hated being short. People would say to my mother, "Don't worry, he'll shoot up"—a phrase that was particularly confusing, since heroin addiction was also a big issue in my neighborhood.)

Howie lived ten blocks away from me, on 180th Street, near the store that sold carrier pigeons. His family rented an apartment over my cousin Jules's barber and beauty supply store, around the corner from my Aunt Bertha. Apparently our baby carriages passed like strange ships in the Bronx sea of humanity, our mothers nodding to each other in casual acquaintance. Howie's mother, Lucille, was a homebody who kept the radio on all day too low to hear but not too low for comfort—a fact I noted with amazement, since background noise was irrelevant for comfort in my family. I thought Howie's mother was a gourmet cook. She mixed garlic powder and Accent into hamburgers. She used the liquid from canned peas when making mashed potatoes. In contrast, my mother relied on tap water, since milk could not be used at meat meals in the kosher tradition. And my mother had not heard of garlic powder, let alone Accent.

I had to keep my mother informed of new culinary developments. I brought Accent into our house, trying to convince myself that the flavor of Mr. Stein's hamburger meat had actually awoken as their ad proclaimed. I persuaded my mother to buy every horror of contemporary advertising, from self-lighting charcoal briquets (we barbecued on the window sill) to Wonder Bread, Bonamo's Turkish Taffy, Twinkies, and Bosco.

Lucille Gelman's hamburgers were perfect circles of meat fabricated by machines at her butcher's. I was impressed. And on Friday nights Howie's father, Jack, arrived home with a confection called "bird's nest," a sort of tangled ribbon of fried dough dusted with powdered sugar. My father never brought food home.

Jack Gelman was an active, bustling man who sported the same crewcut as Howie. He was constantly on the go—repairing electrical things, rigging up pillow speakers, developing his own photographs, taking the family on car outings. Jack might get up on a Sunday morning and decide to drive along the Palisades to see the fall foliage. (At that same moment, my father would be slumped over the *Daily News* or doing laps at the local track.) His idea of fun was to quiz us on our spelling and math. "How do you spell *khaki,* boys?" he would chortle, and when we failed, he would gleefully give us the right answer. He seemed to know so much. I wished he were my father.

Howie's older sister, Sheila, seemed to spend her time talking on the phone and fighting with Jack. Their family represented normality to me—a hearing family that went on outings and had a dog. Howie and I sat and talked for hours. We wrestled endlessly. We speculated on the origin of the universe, on the meaning of life, on paradoxes. (Could God make a rock too heavy for himself to lift?) When Jack bought the *Encyclopedia Britannica,* we pored over it. We read *Mad* magazine and *Superman* comics. Words were things we spun together. And so we passed our time.

I don't recall Howie ever remarking that my parents were deaf. I think he simply accepted it from the beginning, since we were relatively young. As for the other kids in my building, they never seemed to inquire about my parents' deafness. I did feel special because I knew sign language and finger spelling, and I recall teaching Victor Morabito how to finger spell as we sat in the hallway of our building one day. Whereas many children of the Deaf were embarrassed to bring home their friends, I tended to think that my parents' deafness made me special. People usually responded with interest when I mentioned that I knew sign language.

Of course, not everything was rosy, and I'm sure comments were made about my parents behind their backs (and mine). Later, when I was an adolescent, I do recall growing reluctant to bring my friends home. But perhaps that was no more than a sign of the usual teenage repulsion toward any parental domain.

In a kind of wonderful miracle, my mother and Lucille became friends. As a child I took this friendship for granted, but recently I have realized how fortunate it was. Few of my friends who had deaf parents ever experienced that connection with the hearing world. (Jack and my father did not have particularly friendly relations, staying distantly civil for the sake of the boys and the women.)

Howie and I began our friendship in the bathroom of the Hebrew School. When school let out, we would go to the boys' room and linger. We would tell stories, and we would tap dance on the marble floors. People would poke their heads in the bathroom periodically and say, "Are you still here?" But they left us alone, and quickly everyone recognized that we were friends. Now, more than forty years later, Howie is still my oldest and closest friend.

The religious holidays especially brought festivity into my drab world. I loved the commotion that suddenly arose before Passover, with my mother cleaning the house to rid it of any *chumitz* (remnants of leavened bread or things that had touched leavened bread). There was the elaborate taking out the two sets of Passover dishes, used only for one week out of the year. Meats and vegetables that normally appeared on our daily table in culinary street clothes were instead dressed regally. My mother would make matzoh brie and cakes whose lightness was attributable to whipped egg whites only, since leavening was forbidden. (Most of my parents' Jewish vocabulary related either to food or to parental commands. My mother often told me to *Gae schluffen!* [go to sleep].)

The two *seder* nights of Passover were the only annual occasions on which my extended family gathered. I saw my cousins, my distant relatives. The adults sang the interminable prayers; my parents sat at the table unable to follow, amiably silent. The children scampered around, or sat under the table (extended with many wooden leaves) and watched the adult feet. When not praying, the adults stuck to their standard conversations. My mother bustled around, preparing and serving; my father tried to insert his guttural observations amongst the general din. During the reading of the *haggadah,* my parents followed along in the English translations or looked at the pictures, but often they were in the wrong place. I had to help them, even at seven, when I could barely find the place myself.

On Passover my father used to get drunk. He was abstemious throughout the year, but since rabbis over the ages have agreed that celebrants must drink four cups of wine during the *seder,* and since my father did not follow any of the service in Hebrew, he drew companionship from the rabbinical requirements. Four cups later, he was primed enough to sing *Chad Gad Yah* or "One Kid, One Kid," a this-is-the-house-that-Jack-built song about a goat that was killed by a dog who is punished by a farmer and eventually everyone gets killed by the angel of death. It is a kind of funny song that contains grim and reaping reminders about the end of life, the end of the service, and the retributive role of God. Only Jews could end a festival with this musical bad news in comic form. My father stood on wobbly legs and sang in a guttural monotone, testing his own ability to remember the long chain of events. He would stutter, cluck his tongue, and twist his brow into a question that would then break into an expression of enlightenment as he remembered a missing link. He was so comical to us, what with his literally tone-deaf rendition, his wobbly drunkenness, and his absolute determination to finish at all costs. We laughed till the tears came.

❖

Perhaps my most profound schooling occurred at summer camp. I had attended the "mother and children's camp" earlier, but at age nine I went to camp alone. Now that I have my own children, I realize how very young I was to go away from home for three weeks. But a family tradition of going to camp had started with my brother, so I was sent too.

Despite being homesick, I also loved camp. It was, like school, a place to find "normal" parental and fraternal figures who were kind to me, who understood me—who could, at minimum, hear me. My parents (rather, my mother) did not quite understand the importance of nurturing such a young child. Perhaps she did not think I needed much support, so she did not write to me often. In fact, for the first week I received no mail. My counselor became concerned about my sad face during mail distribution and contacted the unit head, who actually called a neighbor to encourage my mother to write. A few days later I received my first letter. It was formulaic, as her letters usually were, but she told me of the mundane goings on in her life, the shopping, visiting, and so on. I was happy about the letter, and although she didn't write as often as the other campers' parents, I did receive one or two more.

The morning group sing embodied everything my life lacked. I do not think I ever sang with people before this moment, aside from droning pointless and boring songs at school. At camp we sang wonderful songs about rising and shining, Noah's ark, climbing Jacob's ladder, being birds in the wilderness, going to magical countries like Oleana, not knowing what to do with drunken sailors, knowing that meetings in buildings would soon be over, that we would overcome, songs filled with strange and lovely words like "kum-bye-yah." Our little voices raised in harmonious thunder, we shivered in the morning chill, watched the mists on the pond, and heard each other coming together into a force larger and more encompassing than any of us singly. At home I had no music; our voices could never be one. So I pitched my heart into those group sings, losing myself in melodious refrains that I understood in sound, if not in word. These were my songs, and music emerged from the silence that had engulfed me for too long.

As we rolled down off the highways, returning to the city, the green began to be replaced by the yellow brick of the apartments and I began to feel sick. Then I saw my mother, smiling and eager to see me. I walked slowly toward her, feeling the camp experience ebbing already. As I kissed her, I felt betrayed by my own feelings of reluctance. I began to regret losing the camp's activities, the friends, the natural beauty.

Somewhere on the trip home, or in our suddenly even more oppressive apartment, I yelled at my mother. Her hovering presence, the absence of any amusement, provoked my rage. Because I had to suppress enormous amounts of frustration, anger then erupted over small things. I could never say to my parents, "Why do I have to come back to this tomb? Why did you have to be deaf? I hate you for being deaf! Let me go back to camp, where I can make copper enamel bracelets and camp out in pine forests!" Instead, I complained about my mother telling me to wash my hands. My mother looked hurt and retorted that, if I was going to act this way, she would not send me to camp next year. It was a hollow threat. I knew nothing could ever keep me from those precious three weeks.

Summer in the Bronx was always unpleasant. Many of my friends were away. I passed the time by throwing my rubber ball against the building and waiting for the heat to build up. Occasionally there would be a stickball or kick-the-can game. If Howie was around, his dad might take us to Orchard Beach or for a weekend barbecue in a park. But the daily heat and boredom were stifling, and the nights were worse.

I was relieved when fall began and I could return to school. My second-grade teacher, Mrs. Berg, was a homely woman who my parents decided might suit Uncle Abie. My father's brother was a squat man with a large cleft in his skull where he had apparently been hit by a falling object when he was young. He was the uncle who was always trying to fix the Emerson console. "Let me just unscrew the back and take a look," he would say. "No!" my father shouted as Abie headed for the sacred object, screwdriver at the ready. Whenever Abie succeeded in entering the television, it was worse for the experience. My parents were on the lookout for a nice woman to succeed his wife, Sally, who had died. Although she was completely unknown to them, Miss Berg seemed to fill the bill because she had those two special qualifications: being Jewish and being unmarried.

Because she was kind to me, Miss Berg was one of those teachers I will never forget. One day she walked me home; on the way she took me to the ice-cream parlor that displayed plaster sundaes and ice-cream sodas in the window. I sat like a prince, eating a sundae and talking to the kindly Miss Berg. In her class I worked very hard on a papier-mâché puppet, and I took great pride in mixing flesh colors myself from red, pink, brown, and blue. It was amazing to me that such different colors could produce a flesh tone.

After Miss Berg there was Mrs. Schecter, followed in fourth grade by Mrs. Gutstein, a relatively young teacher. She was tall, thin, and had a beautiful pony tail. I simply adored her. Consequently, my behavior in class went to hell. I was so desirous of approval that I called out every answer, talked out of turn, and generally made a nuisance of myself. I still got good grades, except a "D" in conduct. I did not care, just so long as I was able to be in her presence each day.

One day, while she was reading us *Mary Poppins,* a man walked into the class, went to the back of the room, and put his feet up on our teacher's desk. It seemed clear that this was Mr. Gutstein. I could pick up on the tension. To exacerbate things, I called out in my brattiest voice, "Mrs. Gutstein, you're blushing!" Her discomfort at her husband showing up in class immediately turned to wrath. I was hauled out of the classroom and chastised severely by my beloved. Later, when I realized that she was in the midst of a divorce, I understood a bit better why she was so upset.

I remember a subsequent encounter with Mrs. Gutstein, when she asked to speak to me as we were leaving the school building. Attempting to salvage a smidgin of masculine dignity for my small self, I turned to her and said, "School's over. I'm on my own time now." And I walked out the door. Perhaps I was still angry at her for the dressing-down? Whatever it was, I know that I was desperately in love with her throughout that year.

The funny thing is that feelings like that do not go unremembered. Years later, in 1968, I was on a bus going down Broadway in Manhattan. I looked out the window to glimpse Mrs. Gutstein among the pedestrians, almost enclosed in a halo of light, as if she were the object of a zoom shot in a film. I had not seen her since fourth grade. I leapt off the bus at the next stop, ran back three blocks, and saw nothing. I was almost convinced that I had hallucinated the event. At that moment she emerged from a bakery. I rushed up to her like a madman, now with student-rebel beard and long hair.

"Remember me? I'm Lenny Davis. Fourth grade? P.S. 92?"

Remembered me? She remembered a lot. It was an incredible moment. There she was, the object of my first preteen love. But now I was a manly eighteen, and she was a youthful thirty-something. For a moment I felt like the hero of a nineteenth-century French novel. She told me she had divorced Mr. Gutstein and now was happily remarried. She wrote her new name and address in a book of haiku that I had with me. I still have the book. When I finally called that number recently, someone else answered.

When I was about nine—perhaps after my solo trip to summer camp?— I began to fear death. When I say "fear death," some will casually register this emotion. Others will assent with profound understanding. There is a fraternity of people who do not know each other but who are bound together by a gut-wrenching, breath-sapping, writhe-inducing anxiety about dying. Emile Zola was one. Of himself and his wife he wrote, "Death has been always in the background of our thoughts, and very often during the night, looking at my sleepless wife, I feel that like me she is thinking of it . . . Oh! It is terrible, that thought—and the terror of it becomes visible! There have been nights when I have leapt suddenly out of bed, for a second or two in a state of abject terror." This dread settles upon the unsuspecting person and grabs the psyche with fierce talons.

The actual moment when I began to fear death is etched in my mind, like a religious edict carved in stone, although the year is not so certain. It was 1957 or 1958. I was in the alleyway of our apartment building talking to David Frietag, whose mother had a concentration camp number tattooed on her arm, and Robin Walvich. Both were a little older than I was. This alleyway, the one in which the feral cats congregated at night, had a netherworld quality, neither street nor building. We thought of it as a dungeon, or tunnel, or mine from whose rough rock we hewed sparkling chips of mica. It was the domain of the dead, the caves of Flash Gordon's clay people. There the fateful conversation occurred.

I had liked David, but in that confusion of early childhood I always associated him with the Nazis. (We used to think *his mother* was a Nazi—the ultimate paradox.) Robin was sitting on a low stone wall that divided our backyard from the next one, and she was telling us how she read about a series of sealed letters by some famous prognosticator, long dead, who had warned his heirs to open each letter on a specific date. The first letter was opened at the turn of the century and correctly predicted the beginning of World War I. The second letter had predicated World War II. The third letter was to be opened in 1960. We all felt sure it would predict World War III.

My entire childhood was affected by the coming of World War III. I had recurring nightmares of nuclear holocaust, of being at school and hearing the sirens, of trying to run home to get to my mother so we could frantically pack our belongings and get to the Short Line bus stop under the Third Avenue El. Then we could take the bus up to the Catskills and stay at my uncle Joe's house to avoid the mushroom cloud and the attendant fallout. Of course, my fantasy involved the idea that I had to save my mother (strangely I never thought about saving my father!), not that she could save me.

The bicycle room in our apartment building suddenly acquired an air-raid shelter sign. It was a small, dank room filled with baby carriages and tricycles. Ironically, it was above ground. There the government planned that I should subsist for months, until the radiation diminished. Live there with the superintendent's family, the old ladies, all the kids? It seemed unimaginable: the blinding flash, the mushroom cloud. Into my generation was instilled the most horrendous sense of insecurity that could be given to a collective childhood. In comparison, the ozone layer's expanding bald spot seems like minor devastation.

So when Robin Walvich predicted World War III, I was visibly terrified. To cheer me up, Robin added the words that sealed my fate: "Don't worry. It will all be over so fast you won't know what happened." This statement inspired no confidence in a child whose only hope is control. The world would end so fast, I wouldn't even know what happened? I couldn't even reach down to get my book bag, let alone get home to my mother? The Short Line to Monticello was clearly beyond possibility. Instead, I would die in a flash. I am not one who rejoices when someone is described as "dying peacefully in her sleep." For my own death, I want to know what is going on.

For some reason the image of people fleeing the molten lava of Pompeii came into my mind at that moment. I must have just seen *The Last Days of Pompeii* starring Basil Rathbone, and the scenes of onrushing lava pouring over screaming extras was burned into my mind and soul. The added irony of Basil Rathbone (really Sherlock Holmes) being trapped in Pompeii and unable to solve the problem made me even more insecure. *You won't know what happened.*

That night I lay in bed after having been tucked in by my father, who routinely accomplished this task with the ritual phrases "Good night, God bless, close eyes; sleep." It was as if he were extinguishing me, rather than making me safe. After he left, I opened my eyes and lay in bed thinking of the end of the world, of the inevitability of death. Suddenly I was seized with a panic that I later came to call "the death vibes." This is the intense and physical realization that you will absolutely cease to be. That there is no exception in your case. That your whole life as lived, all your thoughts and feelings, will have ended, and by ending will never have been. Thus you, and by extension the entire human race, are the butt of a very tasteless joke. These thoughts are accompanied by the deepest chill that can be contained in a human body and by a frantic sense of entrapment. As Zola suggested, the only solution is to jump out of bed in a panic.

I twisted and turned in desperation. I jumped up and ran into the kitchen, where my parents were sitting at the table. I did not confide to them my fears: I simply said I was thirsty. In my family, any fears would be met with "Don't be silly" or the slightly more compelling "Don't worry."

The following nights I was afraid to go to bed. When the lights went out, I knew I would begin to think about the end of the world and about death. I developed an elaborate obsessive behavior, counting every lighted window in the six-story apartment building across the alley from my bedroom. There were about eighty or ninety windows, and I would painstakingly count them. If any of them became illuminated during the counting, I had to start counting all over again. After having counted, I would lie in bed for a few moments, until I saw a light go off or on, at which point I had to recount. The numbers really never came out right, but because I spent all my energies counting, I did not have to stare death in the face. Eventually I just dropped into an exhausted sleep. I arose looking haggard and worn.

I had another method of avoiding thinking about death, by forcing myself to think of the little black cat I had tried to adopt for a day; I would imagine its little face and try to feel its love and warmth. Or I would conjure images of the Sealtest milk carton and the Silvercup bread wrapper. These corporate images of familiar foods gave me emotional sustenance, as if the outside world could beat death through edible consumer products.

I would like to say that I outgrew this fear of death, but it is still inscribed in my being. In recent years, as I approach fifty, I have at least come to better terms with death. I no longer fear it in the way of my youth. This is at least a small accomplishment. The act of writing, the act of remembering, seems in the time-honored sense a way of beating death. Do words live on, as Shakespeare hoped?

> So long as men can breathe or eyes can see,
> So long lives this, and this gives life to thee.

But Shakespeare knew nothing of global warming, nuclear winter, and the curse of entropy.

Are not memory and the fear of death related? I am cursed with memory. As I write, I remember more and more details about my childhood, or I make new connections between things I have known only as separate memories. As Laurence Sterne discovered when he wrote *Tristram Shandy,* the swell of details about a life threatens to obliterate its writing. Some people tell me they cannot remember their lives. I can never forget: forgetting is too close to death. Homer sang of the heroes in order that the memory of them might triumph over their deaths. At the moment of death a Greek soldier achieved his *kleos;* there he triumphed even over the gods, who could never die and thus never achieve that particular glory.

There is a pyrrhic triumph in the remembering that art brings to lived lives. Like my small self, lying in bed at night, hypervigilant, counting lights, trying to take care of myself because no one could hear me, I write my memories. My words are as a stave thrown up into the darkness, a gesture of provisional solidity against all that melts into air.

In a not unrelated phenomenon, I was also about nine when I became the Zenth. The Zenth was my superhero self, the disguise for not-so-mild-mannered Lennard Davis. Garbed in a black cape and black satin mask, he peered out from two lightning-bolt-shaped slits. His mouth appeared through another jagged slash. My mother made these accessories for me, and although the eyeholes were somewhat askew and the cape didn't exactly billow around me, I felt transformed. I concocted the name Zenth from the *Daily News* ads for Zenith televisions. I liked the lightning bolt with which Zenith's first letter was written, but I pronounced Zenith as Zenth. Since no adults could hear my error and correct me, I became THE ZENTH! I ran around the apartment so fast I was simply a blur of black. I saved good people and scourged the bad through my mighty powers and unbelievable strength. And when they asked who had helped them, I laughed a superhero laugh and bellowed: "It's THE ZENTH!"

When I changed back to being Lenny, things were far less interesting, but I knew that I remained just a mask and a cape away from greatness. In my mighty form, no one could harm me. My brother's provocations, my father's scorn, my mother's nervous concern—all fell like broken idols before my wall of strength. I was and would be for all eternity defended, protected, powerful—in short, THE ZENTH, forever triumphant.

Adolescence

And the mists had all solemnly risen
now, and the world lay spread before me.

—Charles Dickens, *Great Expectations*

Distinct moments of experience pre-
ceded my actual teen years. I have two balanced memories related to a
dawning vision of my family's social class. The first is a dim recollection
of a boat ride up the Hudson River. My father worked in the garment
district for a manufacturer of ladies' coats and suits. (I had only a faint
idea of what his work was.) His workshop organized a weekend cruise for
the workers' families. I suppose the International Ladies' Garment
Workers' Union set up the trip, since his employer was not likely that
generous. The boat was rather large, like one of the sightseeing ships that
take people around Manhattan. For this occasion all the men, dark and
hairy, had taken off their shirts so they could bask in their sleeveless
undershirts, their wiry arms, toughened at the sewing machines, extended in athletic ways. The women wore cotton sundresses, and children ran amok. People drank beer, smoked cigarettes, and engaged in a
kind of loud jocularity that is reserved for holidays.

I immediately separated myself from my parents and ran around the deck, dizzy with the feeling of being on the water. I was amazed to see all these people. It gave me a sense that my father actually knew people other than his deaf friends—that his workplace was not just a door he walked through each day, into a blankness that was my absence from him. There was a festivity and a beauty to that ride. As we sailed past the skyscrapers, past the Bronx, and up the river to Bear Mountain, the city dropped away; in its place appeared the silent, gliding greenness of the Hudson River's banks. I suddenly felt part of something larger than myself and my family. Laughter, good-natured kidding, open space— the open, lung-filling space that I had experienced so rarely. At such a moment I felt that life among the urban poor could be more than mere survival in dark, silent, shadowy urban byways.

This positive memory is pierced by a contrasting, more sobering one. One day I happened to go to my father's workplace. (I am not sure how I got there. Perhaps he took me? Or perhaps my mother stopped in to see him?) Nothing had prepared me for what I saw. Certainly, the boat ride up the Hudson had led me to associate life and light with the idea of work. But there before me was a dark, cramped loft filled with men and women hunched over sewing machines. The floor was drab and the varnish, if there had ever been any, had long ago been erased by dragging feet. The walls had achieved that final state of soot-blackened gray brought on by fifty years of inattention. Each worker had a pile of disassembled garments on the left. Each would reach down, pick up a sleeve, attach it to a jacket body, and throw it down on the right. My father was one of these people. I see him sitting by a window that fronted onto a brick wall. He is working in his undershirt on a hot, humid summer day, wearing his reading glasses. He was probably in his early sixties. Around him the (unheard) mechanical din emanated from the rows of sewing machines. Large pressing machines emitted bursts of steam. The ceiling seemed to be laced with hanging cables punctuated by an occasional bare, low-watt light bulb. Other people wheeled bins around and picked up the garment parts.

As my father saw me, he arose with a big smile and hugged me. Because he was delighted to show me off, he introduced me to everyone he could get his hands on.

"My son, Lenny. Say hello to Joe."

"Oh, you're Morris's son. He's something! Does all his work and deaf and all."

"What he say?" my father would sign.

"You deaf and work," I would interpret.

He seemed pleased with the condescending comments, so who was I to tell him not to be? He showed me around, and the more he showed me, the more depressed I got. It was a dark, glum, humiliating place. In my schoolbooks and on television programs, fathers wore suits and sat in their dens. But my father, who could draw English cathedrals with delicate cross-hatchings, who held an American track and field record, who could mime Charlie Chaplin to a tee, was nothing but an indentured servant.

He took me through the doors that separated the workers from the owners. Things were not exactly elegant, even there, but the ambience changed: carpeting, recessed lighting, and secretaries. My father wanted to show me off to the boss.

"Oh, is this your son!" said a bald man with a cigar.

"My son. Say hello to Mr. Carmel."

"So, you're the son. You can hear?"

"Sure."

"Well, your Dad is a really good worker. I can count on him."

"What he say?" my father signed.

"You good worker." Again he was pleased.

"Tell him," my father signed, "You smart boy. Good student. You grow up and become electrical engineer."

This was only one of thousands of moments when my father asked me to tell hearing people things I knew I could not say.

"Tell him," he insisted, exasperation beginning to burn through his facial features.

"I can't," I responded. The boss was still watching but losing interest.

"You ashamed of me?" My father signed.

"No, it's just that . . . "

"Tell him," he said, nudging me forward like a mother dog pushes her pup with a shove of the muzzle.

"My father says I am smart. I'm a good student and I'll be an electrical engineer." I spit out these judgments and predictions like bitter pills.

"Good luck," said the boss, caring not a bit.

My father smiled in delight at my transmission of his great expectations.

A few years ago I had a dream that it was another Great Depression and I had lost my job. Luckily, I was picked out from among the crowd of jostling men seeking work, and I found myself going upstairs in a factory. I was seated at a sewing machine. I picked up some fabric and began to sew. I said to myself, "This isn't so bad." Then I realized that I had the whole rest of the day to sew. And the next day. I woke up and cried for myself, for my father, for all the people who work in factories where they have no say.

My father never seemed to mind. He was proud of his ability to work. He never said he disliked his bosses. As he never complained about his deafness, he never complained about his lot in life. That was not his way. His way was to glorify what he did. He was the best worker, skilled in his craft. I have no doubt that he was.

The older I got, the more my father became a problem for me. Our apartment had only one bedroom, a living room, and a kitchen. The place seemed to belong to him. Somehow this domination of space coalesces into a specific scene, focused, of course, around the Emerson console. In this age before captioned TV shows, he was often mystified by the plot. To compensate he would try to figure out relationships. He would ask me, "Father? Uncle? Who he?" He was always confused as to whether people were married, dating, cousins, or siblings. He was also determined to identify all actors as either Jewish or not. He would point to an actor and, with a quizzical look, make the sign for "Jew" (the right had goes to the chin and strokes an imaginary beard). He would point in delight to another actor and say, definitively, "Jewish!" His entire aim in watching television was to divide the thespian world along religious lines. Any time I watched television with him, I was constantly interrupted with "He is Jewish! She's not Jewish. Is she his wife? Who is the son?" Caught between different anthropological taxonomies, I would stoke a slow burn. And if my father fueled this fire by asking me some trivial question precisely at the most exciting moment in "Perry Mason," just as the murderer jumps up in the courtroom and confesses, I would explode in rage. To anyone who has not grown up in this situation, it might seem cruel to refuse to explain a whodunit to a poor deaf man. But to me, at that moment, it was the last straw of demand heaped on an already tottering tower of responsibilities. From television I sought sweet oblivion, but what I got instead was more interpreting.

So I built myself a tent. It was simple to construct; just take a blanket, tuck it between the wall and the head of the couch, and then under the seat cushions. In that narrow, triangular space I could be free. I would take in my snacks, my reading matter. Through the small opening I could see the television set, but my father could not see me. I could hear him occasionally muttering, "Jewish?" but communication was ruptured. Strangely, he never asked me if I built the tent to escape his questions.

I like to think that in that dark, narrow space I gave myself room to grow into a teenager. But in some ways the tent is a metaphor for how I lived my life. I had to shut out everything around me so I could exist. I could really be myself only in a place to which I could admit no one. This was, and to a certain extent still is, my paradox.

My bar mitzvah marked the end of one life and the beginning of another. I was still very much a boy of the Bronx and my family. I wanted desperately to have a "nice" bar mitzvah. My brother had had a simple reception in the basement of our synagogue, with my father taking box-camera photos. My friends were having catered affairs in rented halls with live music and professional photographers. I cajoled my parents into spending too much money. Of course, we still went tourist class, passing up the country clubs or the Concourse Plaza for Gluckstern's on the Lower East Side. We had to settle on the Crystal Ballroom instead of the Gold or Silver or Diamond one. Instead of a band, we had an accordionist with the requisite pencil-thin moustache. And we had chicken instead of steak. But I was satisfied. We even had a photographer who compiled a gilt-edge album with several novelty photos, including one of my mother and me dancing together superimposed on a page of sheet music for "That Darling Boy of Mine."

I studied for a year in bar mitzvah classes, where I learned to intone by rote the various prayers and readings. Mr. Bald tutored a group of us boys (there were no *bat* mitzvahs for girls permitted in our synagogue) in the lilting, rising and falling tunes that Jews had brought from Eastern Europe. I never felt religiously uplifted. I was simply motivated to be bar mitzvahed—to be a man, as they told me.

On my bar mitzvah day I looked far from manly—tiny and young, as ever. I walked to the pulpit and to Rabbi Paretsky (who bore an uncanny resemblance to Adolf Hitler), where I sang my songs and recited my texts. I even read from a speech that Rabbi Paretsky had written that thanked him profusely, along with my parents. Paretsky thanked me for reading the words he had written in praise of himself. Then he held his hands out over me, saying, "May the Lord bless you and keep you. May He make His face to shine upon you." Odd grammatical constructions always sound particularly religious; still, try as he might, Rabbi Paretsky could not make his own face shine upon me. It sort of scowled upon me, welcoming me to the congregation of men. Two other boys were bar mitzvahed with me, requiring the congregation to sit through an overdose of intoning as each boy recited his set of prayers. I remembered with pride the comment that my brother overheard as he sat next to two old men: one turned to the other and said in Yiddish, "The little one is the best."

Afterward, we adjourned to Gluckstern's, chauffeured exclusively by the IRT subway line past winos and homeless people. The faded elegance of the place was sparked by a garish crystal chandelier that gave the room its name. All my relatives were there, a few I knew well, and many I can barely remember. A moment is frozen in one photograph: a scene in which the bar mitzvah boy blows out the birthday candles, along with his family. I am holding my parents' hands, ready to signal that they are supposed to blow just as the photographer says, "Now." At my own party, I am still interpreting.

A table of deaf friends sits like an island among the hearing. There are the sweet people who have cooed and signed to me since I was a child. They sign and talk, oblivious to the rest. My parents sit with them, rather than the relatives, a true signal of affiliation. Recently, at a family gathering, I asked relatives about my parents. These relatives had assumed that they had done a bang-up job of communicating with my parents, but it was clearly at the most superficial level. They admired my parents for being deaf and still being alive, but they did not really know them.

Adolescence meant blowing open the confines that were becoming too narrow for me. My first attempt was to get a pet. My nurturing instinct went out to every animal I saw. I brought home stray kittens, but my mother always made me put them out because they were "dirty." I would make a bed out of shoe boxes and Kleenex and take the kitten downstairs, putting it in the urine-soaked space under the staircase, envisioning the kitten asleep on its back, paws up over the covers, like a small person. In the morning the kitten was always gone.

I was permitted to have a goldfish. I named it Tommie, after a little boy with polio about whom I had read. I pasted the boy's picture onto the aquarium. But I felt that Tommie was lonely, so I got him a fish companion. On the first night sharing Tommie's tank, the two apparently got into a brawl and the newcomer threw Tommie out of the tank. We found him in the morning on the floor.

I got a turtle, but it developed a soft shell, and I had to flush it down the toilet. By hard coincidence, a few days later I read an article describing a simple way to help turtles harden their shells.

I decided a monkey would be the ideal pet. I read a lot of books, went to the Bronx Zoo, and finally settled on the squirrel monkey—one of those cute, small monkeys whose faces look like little old men with small tufty ears and big eyes. I asked my mother if I could have a monkey. She wearily looked up from her sewing and said, "Ask your father." I asked my father, who was reading the *Daily News*. He said, "Ask your mother." I went back and forth until I received what seemed to me a conditional OK. I proceeded ahead full steam, calling pet stores, reading up on monkey care, and saving my money. Finally I told my parents that I was going to get the monkey.

My mother said, "No, can't have monkey."

"Why not!?"

"Monkey dirty."

"But you said I could!" I responded desperately.

"No, I said ask father."

"But he said I could."

It was to no avail. I was furious. My parents had been too cowardly to express their feelings initially, and now I was hugely disappointed. My whole childhood was a dance with disappointment. My mother would always say to me, "Not get too excited; you disappointed." I was being prepared for a life of limited expectations.

I switched goals. I wanted a parakeet. After all I had gone through, they had to give in. I again called pet stores and found one that had a parakeet. I read books about how to care for the bird. I traveled alone to a pet store in a distant neighborhood. I was only about twelve at the time, and it seemed like a long journey as I rode back on the bus with the bird in a cage on my lap. My parakeet was named Budgie, which is sort of like naming your dog Dog. But I had read in some book that parakeets were called "budgerigars" in Australia. I tamed Budgie, taught him to speak, and even (in reverse lion-tamer action) to put his head in my mouth. That parakeet brought the first (and last) warm-blooded pet into my parents' life. It did them good, particularly my father, who would play with the bird during the long months when he was seasonally laid off from work. I think, in many ways, my whole family relied on me to bring bits of life into the living room.

Budgie met a tragic ending. He developed diarrhea. Having read that one could treat it with antibiotics, I got some Terramycin from the pet store and tried that. It never occurred to me to go to a vet; I didn't have the money, and I didn't know where there was a vet. So I did the next best thing: I went to Dr. Zuckerman, the podiatrist who lived across the landing. As usual, he was in his underwear, wheezing asthmatically. He thought this problem through for a few minutes and advised Pepto-Bismol. He did a quick calculation to reduce the dose to bird-sized proportions and sent me on my way with a dropper. Soon there were pink stains around Budgie's yellow beak and green feathers.

Finally one day Budgie sat in a stupor on his perch. I sensed the end was near. Suddenly he spread his wings and began to flap them slowly, as if he were flying off to the outback. It was an awe-inspiring moment of letting go. Then he folded his wings and fell off the perch with a thud onto the sand-strewn paper at the bottom of his cage. He was no more, probably poisoned by the bismuth in Pepto-Bismol. I wept.

I took him downstairs for a burial, but I could find no dirt—only concrete. So I buried him deep in the garbage cans, hoping the feral cats wouldn't find him. Then I went upstairs and disinfected the cage. I never got another bird.

When I was twelve, I entered Junior High School 44. At the time it had little claim to fame, although after November 1963 we learned that Lee Harvey Oswald had been one of our distinguished alumni. My brother had preceded me there, and I had some of the same teachers. I was in the "SP" class, which was short for "Special Progress." In other words, we took three years of schoolwork in two. I tried to do as well as I could, and I was elected class president, largely on the platform of cuteness. Since I was underdeveloped, many girls voted for me in some tribute to small, soft, cuddly things. I was inducted in the Arista Society, an honor society, and even managed to win the science fair. I did most of what I did with a sense of fraudulence. As class president, I always forgot to attend the few student government meetings that were held—clinging to some notion that cuteness absolved me from participating in the world. As for the science project, I replicated an experiment I had heard on a radio show called "The Science Reporter." The experiment that interested me, as I sat at the Formica kitchen table eating my mother's ersatz chicken chow mein, was one in which planaria (a kind of worm) were given electric shocks coinciding with flashes of light to produce a Pavlovian response. Each time a light was flashed, the worms would cringe. Then, when you chopped up a conditioned worm and fed it to an unconditioned worm, the cannibal instantly learned what his dinner had known.

This controlled sadism appealed to me. I wrote a letter to the professor who had designed the experiment, and I received an offprint of the scientific article. Now I had only to buy some planaria and get myself a strong battery. I misread the size of planaria, "3mm long." I asked my father, who told me they were 3 meters long. Like snakes, I thought, a bit nervously, trying to imagine shocking large serpents in my bedroom. I hauled home an enormous tank from school, only to find when my planaria arrived that they were virtually invisible.

Anyway, I broke the worms up into groups and began conducting experiments in my mother's soup bowls. These were not ideal containers: the water tended to evaporate, leaving behind small, dried shards of worms. After my control group died, I had to take other worms, already conditioned, to be in the control group. Eventually I completely lost track of which worms belonged in which group. Nevertheless, I prepared brilliant illustrations and called my project "How to Make a Memory Pill." My exhibit featured a small petri dish with aspirin to look like "memory pills"; kids would ask me if these were the real pills. I ended up going to the New York City science fair and winning third prize. I was on television and in the newspapers, fraudulently bearing my banner of greatness. I still have the stopwatch I won.

When it came time to go to high school, I discovered that my options were limited. My brother had gone to the Bronx High School of Science, and I was expected to do likewise. But I decided I would also try for the High School of Music and Art. This was where all the cool, bohemian types went. As usual, I had to go to the interview by myself, on the City College campus in Harlem. I took the subway to a stop at 145th Street and had to walk seven or eight blocks, lugging my giant art portfolio. I made it to the school in good shape, took their art test, showed my work, and then headed home. I returned to the subway stop, but as I was paying my fare, a group of older African American boys started harassing me. They asked me for money. I took advantage of a momentary pause and slipped through the turnstile, assuming they would not follow, but they did. I went down to the first level in the subway. Again they surrounded me.

"Give us all your money," one said bluntly.

I thought for a moment, always assuming that I could talk myself out of a difficult situation, then I said, "What's money?"

There was a puzzled instant, then one of them said, "You know, money—dollars, cents."

"Sorry," I replied trying to keep cool, "I don't know what money is."

Again I took advantage of confusion to slip away to the next, lower level of the subway, hoping the train would come. But it didn't, and again I was surrounded. Again they demanded money, and again I pretended I came from a nonpecuniary domain. Finally, in exasperation, one of the boys took something from his pocket and put it behind his back.

"Do you know what I have behind by back?" he asked me.

"No," I said in a less confident voice.

He pulled it out with a flourish. It was a bottle of Old Spice aftershave lotion. My brother had a bottle too, and there were endless commercials on television with the jingle "'Old Spice means quality,' said the captain to the boatswain. Look for the bottle with the ship that sailed the ocean."

While I was pondering the jingle and wondering why I was being accosted with a bottle of aftershave, the boy smashed the bottle against the metal pillar next to me. I looked at the jagged edges of glass.

"You know what I'm going to do with this?"

I shook my head.

Then he took the bottle, inverted it over me, and poured the contents on my head. The cloying liquid was quickly absorbed by my thick wool coat. I stood there reeking in a way that both the captain and the boatswain might have found offensive.

After a long pause, I looked the boy right in the face and said, "So, now I smell nice."

Another long pause. Then he reached down and put his arm around me.

"Hey, you got heart!" he nodded approvingly.

The other boys slapped my back and hand saying, "He's got heart. He's OK." Then they walked off.

When I got on the train, all noses turned toward me. I never forgot this moment, when the power of words extricated me from a potentially dangerous situation.

But I couldn't talk myself out of destiny. I was fully expected, as a smart kid in the SP class, to go to Bronx Science. The specialized school required passing a difficult entrance exam. My parents simply assumed that I would follow in my brother's footsteps; so did my teachers. But when I went to take the exam, I fell into a kind of reverie. In a matter of minutes, it seemed, the test was over. I was not sure if I did well, poorly, or was even there for the exam.

One day our guidance counselor came into the social studies class and announced; "Children, I have the results of the Science test. I will call the names of the students who got in. When I do, will you please stand?"

I kept waiting for my name to be called, but after the last-named child rose, I realized that I had failed. All of the seated children looked at each other in dismay, while the standing ones bore broad grins of triumph. I slunk home, realizing for the first time that a single decision can shape one's life.

My teachers were all upset, and they called the Science school. I was put on a waiting list, but I never got in. So now my choices for high school were limited severely. I did gain admission to Music and Art, but

I felt I wanted a more academic path. The local high school, Roosevelt on Fordham Road, had a bad reputation. The only alternative was to enroll in a special program at De Witt Clinton High School. It was billed as a "Scholarship" program, above the honors program, but I was dubious. At least Howie would be going with me.

De Witt Clinton's motto, *sine labore nihil* (Without Work, Nothing), was suited to inculcate working-class submission. When I attended, it housed six thousand boys from the Bronx, only a fraction of whom were in the honors or scholarship programs. The rest were there to get by at best and make trouble at worst. My only consolation was that, since we shared a bus stop and a playing field with Bronx Science, the truly bad boys of my school would exercise their sadistic impulses on the nerdy, slide-rule-carrying kids from Science, rather than on me. My Clinton jacket, in black and red, protected me from violence out of some distorted sense of school loyalty on the part of bullies.

As I grew older, I began to want to move out of our neighborhood. Gangs like the Fordham Baldies, who wore Mohawk haircuts and who sandpapered people's faces, terrorized the streets. Jews and the Italians were slowly being displaced by Latinos and African Americans. My parents were not openly bigoted, and (to their credit) they espoused equality when called upon to do so; still, there was a subtle message that "colored people" and "Puerto Ricans" were not our kind. Rather than seeing themselves as part of a marginalized group, my parents saw themselves as white and as part of the hearing world—although who could have been more of a minority than deaf, working-class Jewish immigrants in the Bronx?

I had no way of understanding class and power, except by an instinctive resentment and embarrassment about my lot in life, and I saw the influx of poor immigrants as the sign of a deteriorating neighborhood. My friends were moving, preferably to Queens, or best of all Forest Hills, which sounded very bucolic. Barring that, to Pelham Parkway, or even the Grand Concourse. Anything sounded better and greener than Clinton Avenue.

To move meant fleeing the poverty that deafness brought. My humiliation was not so much about my parents' physical difference but, on a concrete level, how that translated into the neighborhood and the apartment. I was old enough now to have visited friends from summer camp. Some of them lived in relatively luxurious houses in the suburbs, as did some of my relatives. When I returned home, I saw my shabby, grim, cramped quarters. I remember my brother bringing home his fiancée from Long Island, and her saying that our apartment was "quaint."

I had to get out. If my parents did not want to move, I would move them anyway.

When I was thirteen, I began to look at alternative housing. By this time my brother had married and moved to Forest Hills, where he lived in a one-bedroom apartment in a luxury high-rise called Parker Towers. I combed the classified ads each day, seeking an apartment we could afford in a "better" neighborhood. Somehow I got a list of middle-income cooperatives that the state was subsidizing. I made phone calls and decided to look at one in Pelham Bay. I remember taking a very long subway ride with my mother to stare at the rubble of a building under construction. Based on a quick walk around, we decided against this choice, since it was not very different from where we already lived.

Then I found out about Concourse Village, a giant development near Yankee Stadium. We could afford a two-bedroom apartment there. I desperately wanted two bedrooms, even though my parents had given me the bedroom and were sleeping in the living room. And I liked the idea of living near the Grand Concourse; it seemed so elegant, with its wide boulevard built in deliberate homage to the Champs Élysées. There was also Jamaica Village in Queens. Finally we (or was it I?) decided on Nagle House, a building in the Inwood area of upper Manhattan. This as yet unbuilt middle-income cooperative was perched on a granite outcropping right next to the elevated train tracks. (Somehow that juxtaposition did not disturb me.) I had a special attraction to the neighborhood because my class had once taken a trip to Inwood Park to look at Native American caves and stand on the very site where Manhattan was supposedly purchased for the famous trinkets. Some friends and I had later returned to the area because we liked the park. We also discovered that attractive blonde Irish girls lived in that neighborhood. Our visits had become more frequent and elaborate as we discovered that we could walk down the Hudson River by the railroad tracks and then cross the George Washington Bridge on foot and climb down the Palisades, where we could swim in the river. Howie, Aaron Zaretsky (a friend from summer camp), and I would descend the rocks on the Manhattan side of the Hudson, perching precipitously over the cars barreling down the West Side Highway. In fact, once Howie got stuck on a narrow outcropping and could move neither up nor down. After harrowing minutes, we managed to talk him through a complex maneuver and prevent him from being a horrible news story the following day. We never told our parents what we did on our adventures.

These trips made me like the Inwood area, and although my parents had absolutely no connection to that neighborhood, I was the one who was finding places and making decisions, so I convinced them that we should move. We could only afford a one-bedroom apartment, without a balcony. But the neighborhood was safer, closer to the Palisades and to the Irish girls. We were across the street from a low-income housing project, but that did not bother me, because a few kids I knew lived there.

We had to wait a year for the building to be built. Finally, one day we received a letter announcing a meeting of the future cooperators to be held in the Y on Nagle Avenue. My mother and I attended. (My father, other than paying the down payment, was not involved in any aspect of this move.) I was thrilled to be moving soon and to see who was going to share our new building. My mother dressed up nicely.

As we arrived people were filing in the room. Almost everyone was African American. This was a big shock for my mother. "Everyone colored!" she said, using the old, racist sign for "negro" (middle finger touching the nose). My feelings were mixed. I could see that the future tenants of Nagle House seemed nice and polite, but I also felt responsible for my mother's discomfort. How was I to know that the people moving into the Irish neighborhood would be black?

When we went home, my mother cried. I tried to explain the civil rights movement to her, all the while being a bit uncertain myself. It was too late to pull out. My mother stood around for months with her arms crossed, thinking and worrying. She would tell me that her stomach was all aflutter. There is a deaf sign in which the fingers of both hands are frozen into a position as if one had just been clawing at something; then these clawlike hands are moved in agitated circles over the stomach. This sign means discomfort, agitation, nervousness, or even unsettled digestion. Despite her reservations, we moved.

Being in Nagle House was a wonderful experience for me. While some white tenants canceled their leases as a result of the meeting at the Y, the ones who stayed were good folks. I had the opportunity to spend my teen years among a truly integrated group of kids. (Ironically, the white kids were integrating the predominantly black building.) At first, the Irish people who lived in the neighboring apartment building were not so happy. They had tolerated for years living across the subway tracks from a low-income housing project, but they were clearly distressed that the new high-rise on their own side of the tracks was filled with blacks. Gunshots were fired into our building and offensive graffiti appeared. But gradually, over the year, we all were accepted as inevitable, if not really welcomed.

I became very involved in the cooperative, writing a teen column in the newsletter and serving as the teen member of the board of directors. This required passing some state-mandated test, and I felt for the first time in my life somehow approved of and effective in an institutional setting. I spoke for the teenagers. My father also became active. He was a wonderful artist, and his drawing of the building was adopted as the official logo for the coop's letterhead. He also wrote a newsletter column in which he interviewed people in the building—an incredible act of self-confidence for a deaf man. Despite the fact that the IRT subway ran past our building every five or ten minutes, often rendering inaudible key scenes in television shows, I was content. Of course, the elevated train was a non-problem for my parents.

Quiet is terribly important to me now; I would never live near a train or even a bus line. I must simply have adopted my parent's deafness while I was living with them. I was happy to reside in a brand-new apartment with no roaches or rodents, with a new paint job and no cracks in the plaster, and with a continuous supply of hot water. If I craned my head, I could see the sun setting over the Palisades. True, I was still in a one-bedroom apartment with my parents, but I felt safer in this neighborhood. Despite the gunshots.

A tall, excruciatingly thin African American fellow who played piano at church lived across the hall from me. He and I traveled together to high school everyday. I was also friends with a girl named Jeanie, whose father was the kind of alcoholic who was never drunk but always had the sweet smell of wine on his breath.

I came to be closest with a pair of sisters named Barry and Ray. Their father was a school principal. (The African American tenants were more upwardly mobile and professional than the whites, who tended to be bus drivers or plumbers.) Barry was my age, and I quickly fell in love with her. She and her sister lived a kind of intellectual, bohemian life to which I aspired. There were more books in her house than just *Hello the Boat* and *Lad: A Dog,* and she named her pet gerbil Voulu, in French the past tense for "want." We spent much time together and talked about literature, art, poetry, and music. This was when Bob Dylan was going electric and the Beatles had come out with *Rubber Soul.* I don't think we ever kissed, but things felt very warm and intimate. When I went to camp that summer, Barry sent me a letter in which she said she wanted to marry me. I did not really understand her meaning, and I wrote her back a poem about a moth that is drawn to the upper atmosphere in search of the moon and so asphyxiates. I still have her letter, and when I read it recently, I realized it was asking me to have sex with her. I had been too inexperienced to understand her desire.

In the building we had a rec room for the teens. We scrounged up an old stereo and even a pool table, books, and chairs, although we never succeeded in making the room cozy. An adult named Keith, who was a social worker, was our advisor. He loved jazz, and so we listened endlessly to Miles, Coltrane, and all the others. I learned to play pool, and we had dances. Kids from the neighborhood came, mainly from the housing project across the tracks, including Lew Alcindor, later to be known as Kareem Abdul-Jabbar. He was so tall that he had to duck to come through the door; when he danced with a girl, it was like watching a giraffe dance with a poodle.

At Nagle House I came into my own self. I read *Catcher in the Rye* and *Death Be Not Proud* and decided I was a rebel with a brain tumor. I started to wear tight black jeans and bought a pair of granny sunglasses. I wrote my first poem on my own— "Sonnet from Youth to Age," about my relationship with my father. It began with the line "My time about to come and yours just passed." I sent the poem to the *New Yorker*, which responded with what I thought was a very nice rejection slip. I wrote another poem about the tension of a thunderstorm building up but not coming. I remember running around the cramped apartment alone one afternoon after school, feeling the negative ions of the impending storm; or was I just feeling some unnamed sexual tension? The poem ended with "hate, heat, away . . . " I started to play the guitar and wrote Dylanesque songs with lines like "Men take others to be enslaved, / Others say they want to be saved." I wrote a short story about a teenager who had a fantastic room in a huge house. The room was a jungle of giant plants, and all kinds of wild animals lived in it as pets.

I desperately wanted my own room. At this point my mother slept on the folding couch in the living room, and my father and I slept on single beds in the bedroom. The rationale was that my mother needed to go to bed earlier than my father and me, since she had to get up earlier to go to work. As for their sex life, I must have assumed it no longer existed. My father told me later—in an airport, as was his inappropriate way, to make strange admissions in public places—that he would sneak out in the middle of the night to my mother, who would sign to him, "OK, OK, come on."

My father had the annoying habit of sucking on his teeth, presumably to get out all remnants of food. Of course, he could not hear himself and so made many noises—embarrassing to me, of course, but not to him. At this age I wanted privacy, and all I got was two hours after school until my parents arrived home (provided that my father was working and not at home during one of his seasonal layoffs, when he would sit on the couch reading the *Daily News*). Those two hours were my own. I found a stash of *Playboys* in the incinerator room and used them in the unimaginative ways of teenage boys. I was alone to do whatever adolescent things I needed to do. But then, at night, I was constrained by my father's hemming and hawing.

When the lights were turned off, I would lie in bed and wait. He would begin to suck on his teeth with long, high-pitched intakes of air. The sounds were both squealing and moist. They crawled into my unconscious and reminded me of the sucking sounds of my parents' lovemaking. In my adolescent state of contempt and exasperation, I would lie in bed trying to block out the sounds. I would turn up my transistor radio to drown him out, but his sounds would pierce through the music.

Finally one night I could stand it no longer. I leapt out of bed and began pounding on his chest. He, of course, was startled. I turned on the light and began to scream, "Stop making noise! Drive me crazy!" I signed frantically. To his credit, he did not yell at me or punish me. He must have sensed how fragile was the dam restraining my emotions.

My only salvations were school, summer camp, and the library. There was a branch of the public library in my neighborhood and another on Fordham Road. I spent hours browsing the shelves without any instruction or advice. One book I picked up was *Portrait of the Artist as a Young Man* by James Joyce. Actually, as I was rummaging through the shelves I saw *Ulysses* and read the prologue about the obscenity trial. I was intrigued by the fact that Joyce's work was considered obscene but was also in my library. I checked out the shorter book and read it, and then I read *Ulysses*. I was confused, of course, but my high school English teacher, Ronald Greenhouse, helped me to understand things. I was impressed with myself for reading the book, but I was also impressed with the book. When I saw in *Ulysses* the term "LSD" I was intrigued: Did they have that drug in Ireland at that time? I asked Mr. Greenhouse, who went to look up the allusion in his glosses and came back with the analysis that "L" was Leopold and the "SD" was Stephen Dedalus; also the "L" might stand for "Lunch," since it was in the chapter when Bloom goes to lunch. But my father, looking over my shoulder told me matter-of-factly that it stood for "pounds, shillings, and pence." Despite his grade-school education, he was right.

When I was in high school my father decided that it was time to talk with me about sex. I remember one night when he and I were on the subway and I was studying my advanced biology textbook. As he peered over at the diagrams, something tripped his associative memory and he asked me if I knew about sex. Since my brother had taken out the zoology textbook when I was younger and explained everything he could to me, I felt I knew the ins and the outs of the subject. I tried to prevent my father from telling me about sex on the subway, with the prying eyes of the hearing watching over us, but he was unstoppable.

Another time we were at home, so I had to listen to his advice. His wisdom came filtered through his deaf-school experience and the Edwardian era in which he reached consciousness. (He was born in 1898.)

"First thing," he raised his teaching forefinger to emphasize. "Always remember: syphilis, gonorrhea very painful!" Pronouncing "gonorrhea," he placed the emphasis on the second syllable and rumbled around the consonants. Even so, I understood. His face twisted into the living expression of pain, which instantly made me feel that he himself had been afflicted. "Very painful!" he emphasized again, signing the word for pain (two fingers pointing to each other and vibrating with electric intensity). "Suffer," he signed (the two fingers turning into clenched fists slowly rotating around each other).

"Very careful when go with women." I nodded, although the idea of "going with women" in that way seemed remote, rather as if he had warned me about climbing Mr. Everest. "Some women tell you, 'I am clean.' Don't trust. No woman clean." My father's advice was beginning to sound a bit fishy, particularly since he was always washing his hands. And what about my mother? Wasn't she clean?

"Never sex with promiscuous women." The rules were raining down from on high. My brain was racing to understand. "Promiscuous women bad. Not clean." OK, I was thinking. What exactly was a promiscuous woman? A woman who wanted to have sex. Was that bad? After all, this was the mid-sixties. Were the Beatles singing about promiscuous women? That term seemed strange, but not as strange as what followed. "Avoid promiscuous women; always go to prostitutes." Ah! That was the answer. The reasoning was impeccable: "You have sex with promiscuous women, they say they clean. No woman clean. With prostitute must take precaution. Know *not* clean!"

I suddenly conjured an image of my father from a photograph. He was in London dressed in dapper clothing, his hat at a rakish tilt. It was the 1920s, and he was standing with a woman who was not my mother. She had on a coat with a fur collar and wore a flapper hat. Another couple stood next to them, equally dressed to the nines. Were these promiscuous women? Had my father learned the hard way to stick to the safe road of prostitutes?

The next piece of advice: "Always use condom." I was wishing that he would stop. "And when you finish condom," he said, winding up his lesson with that supreme moment of wisdom passed on from father to son, "Always wash condom out before use it again!" This advice was consonant with my father's favorite alliterative motto: "Willful waste makes woeful want." I can't say that I lived up to his counsel, but I never forgot it.

It was 1965, and the world began to open up for me. Although I lived in the stifling confines of my parents' home, where the same routine events happened with the same tedium, I began to experience New York City. This was the time of the civil rights movement and the antinuclear, antiwar campaign. My first introductions to these forces happened through the intercession of an art counselor from summer camp, Mary, who was a student at Columbia University. She asked Howie and me if we wanted to join her on a march for jobs, peace, and freedom. This was a very exciting prospect. I asked my parents if I could go, and they agreed. The neglect I had suffered in my early childhood began to appear, in adolescence, more desirable. My parents often let me do what I wanted, assuming that I knew more about the world than they did. As a young teenager, I had the run of the city.

That Saturday morning Howie and I met Mary at her apartment near Columbia. This was the first time I had been in an apartment not owned by a parent. Mary had set things up very nicely, but what I remember most was that she had a double bed. This seemed like a quiet statement of maturity. I longed for the day when I would have my own double bed and apartment. We went with her to her biology lab, saw her dissected dogfish, and then ended up marching with the Columbia contingent that assembled in front of the Chock Full O'Nuts on 116th Street and Broadway, opposite the campus gates. We marched and chanted en route to the United Nations.

The experience led me to others like it. My friend Aaron Zaretsky's family was much more socialist than mine. His brothers, one of whom was Eli Zaretsky, now a well-known Marxist sociologist, espoused leftist causes, and through him I started working for CORE (Congress on Racial Equality). I used to stand all day at the corner of Eighth Street and Sixth Avenue in Greenwich Village with a coffee can in hand, collecting donations and getting people to sign petitions.

My life expanded further. I discovered that if I took a zero-period gym class, I could get out of school at one in the afternoon. The city became my school. I would take the subway down to either Central Park or the Museum of Modern Art. At the museum I would wander around, usually ending up at *Guernica* or some surrealist painting. Then I would see a film at their cinémathèque. I learned instinctively about modern art and cinema. I probably saw more silent films—the works of D. W. Griffith, F. W. Murnau, and Fritz Lang—than any other high school kid. I spent a lot of time in the museum cafeteria, desperately hoping to meet a young woman who would match my artistic and intellectual desires—some long-haired, leotarded artist with Fred Braun sandals. I never succeeded, although I ended up meeting many interesting people. Most notably, one day when I was reading a book, a man approached me and said, "I entirely disagreed with what you wrote." I had no idea what he was talking about. "What you said about photography was all wrong." It took me a few minutes to make clear that I was not who he thought I was. It turned out he mistook me for A. D. Coleman, the photography critic for the *Village Voice*. The fellow standing before me was Todd Papageorge, an up-and-coming photographer. After the misunderstanding was cleared up, Todd invited me over to his table, the regular meeting spot for many famous New York photographers. So this became my table, where the great Museum of Modern Art photographers hung out. I listened to Gary Winograd and others discuss their Leicas and Hasselblads as I drank my coffee and ate my danish.

By now my brother was living in Forest Hills with his wife, Gail, a vivacious twenty-three-year-old. Her father was a radio announcer, and there was showbiz in her ways. I was surprised that my staid brother had married such a comedienne. My brother was in advertising now, and they had moved into a "luxury" high rise where Rocky Graziano, the prize fighter, was also among the occupants. I was impressed.

My parents and I would go out to the suburbs to visit with Gail's parents. I could not imagine a greater contrast. Although their house was modest, to me it seemed like Mansfield Park. We would sit in their yard, have drinks, and eat strawberries picked from their garden. Gail's mother was on Valium, a sign of upward mobility to me. Her father looked like a cross between Steve Allen and Robert Goulet. And Gail had a sister who was a few years older than I. Susan was tall and willowy, an equestrian. I felt like Pip visiting Estella. In some way she seemed destined for me, and the symmetry of brother marrying brother's wife's sister was arresting. I fell a bit in love with her and found myself tongue-tied, but always knew the impossibility of the match. Gail had much of the bad girl in her. She would go out and spend $400 on a pair of shoes. She was employed as receptionist at Ashley Famous, the talent agency. Once, when I was leaving the Museum of Modern Art, I stopped in to see her. It was after hours, and she was alone with a man who seemed quite interested in her. It turned out to be William Shatner, who poked me in the stomach a few times and then suggested I look through a telescope at the neighboring Hilton to see some nude guest.

Gail had a way of taking me aside and whispering in my ear, "I like you better than your brother." As a sixteen-year-old this disoriented me, but as a narcissist I thought she was right. Once, when I was home alone with her, she asked me to lie down next to her on the bed. I was so inexperienced in these things, I felt uncomfortable and confused. She must have realized that I was not going to be her male Lolita, and she made no further requests. A few years later, she and Gerald were divorced.

Typically, I told no one about this encounter. I really had no way to understand what was going on. This inchoate, unnameable quality to my emotional life, the isolation I experienced, was so pervasive that I never noticed it.

8

College and Other Awakenings

... he moved along the level way between pollard willows growing indistinct in the twilight, and soon confronted the outmost lamps of the town [Christminster]—some of those lamps which had sent into the sky the gleam and glory that caught his strained gaze in his days of dreaming, so many years ago. They winked their yellow eyes at him dubiously, and as if, though they had been awaiting him all these years, in disappointment at his tarrying, they did not much want him now.

—Thomas Hardy, *Jude the Obscure*

More than any other single experience, college led me to realize the strengths and limitations of my upbringing. My feelings about being poor, from a "bad" neighborhood, and from a Deaf family had all been fairly inchoate; likewise my feelings of resentment and any dawnings of political consciousness. My parents were good working-class folks who accepted their social position as they accepted their deafness. They bought into the dominant ideology and decided it was more practical to salt their food than rue their portion. I believed I was savvier, cooler, and more down-to-earth than any rich kid—not that I'd met any, other than my cousin Lori from the Concord Hotel.

But college comes to teenagers as a tangible and unavoidable reminder of what is no longer possible to finesse through charm, wit, or simple denial. College involves absolutes: SAT scores, ability to pay, social class, and alumni connections.

When it came time for college, I was more than ready. My brother had lived at home and attended City College. I was determined not to follow in his footsteps. I yearned to leave home. The narrow circle of my parents' lives and the stifling surroundings of my neighborhood made flight the only option.

The way out was through the College Office at De Witt Clinton High School. This office was Doc Bernhard's personal fiefdom. Doc apparently never taught a class other than elocution, where we learned to say "vanilla" instead of "vanella," "chocolate" instead of "chawklet," and pronounce the "u" in "duty" so it didn't sound like dog excrement—all this so we could escape the telltale accents of our plebeian origins. I thought Doc was a genius because he had written an entry in the *Encyclopædia Britannica*. He lived in a fancy suburb, I imagined, and used his office and our student assistance to run a program called Bernhard Tours, under whose aegis he escorted wealthy girls through Europe. My job was to run off his travel brochures on the mimeograph machine.

Doc decided to which colleges we should apply: in my case, Oberlin, Princeton, Columbia, and Harpur College (the undergraduate division of SUNY/Binghamton, where I currently teach). My parents balked at the cost of applying anywhere but City College and refused to let me apply out of state. I didn't really want to go to Oberlin. I had only the fuzziest of ideas of what a college other than City College might be like, but I knew I should apply to the places Doc had advised. I told my parents I would pay for the applications out of my bar mitzvah money, but they said no.

As the battle mounted, I determined to run away. I packed my chinos, took the E train to Forest Hills, and stayed with my brother. I planned to stay a while, but my parents caved in all too quickly and let me spend my money on prospects in Ohio.

My Princeton interviews were nightmarish. I had a preliminary interview with a businessman alumnus at 666 Fifth Avenue. Although I was not then aware of the significance of the numerical mark of the beast, I have come to see that this address was not accidental.

I was familiar with the neighborhood since the Museum of Modern Art was just around the corner. I put on my herringbone sports jacket (I had bought it at Robert Hall, a discount clothing store, trying to imitate my English teacher's tweediness at a bargain price) and set out. In a certain sense this journey paralleled my hapless foray into Harlem for my interview at the High School of Music and Art. Only now I would be mugged by the gentry.

Waiting in the spacious outer office, I observed the conspicuous self-importance of the Alumnus. Then I was ushered into an even larger office overlooking Fifth Avenue. The Alumnus was tall, WASPish, conservative. I was in unfamiliar territory, far from my parents' sweatshops. I felt uncomfortable.

"So, you want to go to Princeton?"

"Yes."

"And you come from . . . " He squinted at a piece of paper. "De Witt Clinton High School in the Bronx?"

He might as well have said Harlem or Watts or Flatbush. I was not the typical Princeton entrant. At that age I was beginning to signal my affiliation with what would be called the counterculture. The Alumnus quickly moved to a topic that would flush out my traitorous attitudes.

"What do you think of this fellow burning himself in front of the UN?" He was referring to an antiwar protestor. I rose to the bait.

"I think he has a right to do that if he opposes the war."

The Alumnus saw blood in my answer.

"But suicide is against the law. He broke the law to make his protest. Do you favor breaking the law to make a protest?" He was practically yelling at me, glowering from behind his mahogany desk while I receded into my low chair.

"Well," I retorted, "He was punished by his own death."

"Against the law!" Alumnus shouted like a righteous preacher. "If everyone burned themselves to protest a cause, where would we be?"

"We'd be fine," I said. "We'd be out of this ridiculous war."

"You're against the war?" Alumnus bellowed. "Do you want the

Communists to take over Southeast Asia? Then it's just a quick hop to the rest of the world."

"Domino theory," I thought. I had been reading *Time* magazine, just as he had. But instead of responding, I become aware of a strange whirring sound.

I said, speaking over the noise, "How do you know that would happen? Don't the Vietnamese have a right to elect their own . . . " My voice faded as the whirring sound increased. The room began spinning slowly, and the whir became deafening. Soon even he noticed my ashen countenance.

"Are you OK?" he asked, "You look pale."

"I'm not feeling very . . . "

I sat in the chair for a long time, on the verge of fainting or vomiting. Finally, realizing that it would be a bad idea to do either on a college interview, I managed to pull my brains and rising gorge into line. The whirring slowed, then stopped.

I remember little else, except limply offering my clammy hand for the Alumnus's beefy, firm grasp. I experienced a general sense of failure, a feeling of victimization and injustice that tethered me to my neighborhood and my parents. I was different from the kids who would enter the Ivy League. I didn't really belong at a place like Princeton. I walked down into the subway, reassuming my subterranean position in society, and slunk home.

My actual visit to Princeton was equally mystifying. The City College campus was the one with which I was most familiar, centrally located in Harlem at 138th Street and Convent Avenue. There one could see a few Oxford-aspiring buildings and perhaps a few vines of ivy. I also used to glance into the Fordham University campus on my way to Alexander's Department Store. I was not prepared for the picture-book splendor of Princeton.

I boarded at the grimy George Washington Bridge terminal and sat by myself as the bus wound its way through the industrial nightmare of New Jersey. I debarked at pristine Princeton and found my way to the admissions office. As I wandered through the parklike grounds, seeing the blue-blazered collegians and the august buildings, I had a profound sense of being an outsider. I remember that even the squirrels were different: all black. These were just about the only blacks on campus at the time.

Some nondescript professional-managerial person interviewed me. All I recall was that he commented, "I notice there is a dramatic skewing of your board scores. How do you account for that?"

"I'm not very good at math."

"Apparently," he said humorlessly.

When I took my campus tour, I learned that chapel attendance was mandatory. I was told I would join a club where I would eat with other chapel-going young men. Oh yes, there was a synagogue as well; I could attend those services if I chose. I tried to imagine myself fitting in and could foresee massive depression or rebellion as my only options. I took the bus back, vaguely relieved to see the squalor of New York City, feeling as if I were returning from fast-fading Brigadoon. My parents didn't even ask me what happened.

My interview at Columbia was better. At least the university had a stop on my usual subway line, and I had already been there when I had gone on the civil rights march. However, things got off on the wrong foot—literally. I mistakenly exited at a subway stop six blocks away. It was raining torrentially. My herringbone sports jacket soaked up the drops as I walked. On the campus at last, I slipped and fell on the slick bricks that lined College Walk, smearing mud on my pants. At the interview I was dirty, wet, and prepared for further humiliation.

Irwin Glickes, a dean and member of the English Department, interviewed me. The conversation went well. I remember that when he asked if I had any questions, I pulled out a sheaf of index cards. He joked by saying, "I wish I had the answer cards." Columbia invited me back for a reception designed to impress the preferred candidates. Arthur Danto, the philosopher, addressed us and told us about wonderful ideas that other people had thought. He drew a circle on the blackboard and said that knowledge was like the circle, and the unknown was what was just outside the circle. The larger the circle of what you knew, the greater the contact with what you didn't know. The more you learned, the more ignorant you were. I thought this was profound—certainly much smarter than the information I was gleaning from my economics class at Clinton, where I was learning about limited partnerships. Despite Danto's paradox (or because of it), I wanted to learn, to have my circle grow and grow. I wanted to be part of a vast archive of knowledge.

Danto's eye was not on me but turned inward. I remembered that, in Renaissance art, philosophers were often painted with inward-turning eyes, symbolic of their thoughtful natures. I wrote a letter to Dean Glickes afterward, telling him that I wanted to be part of an "intellectual community." People like Arthur Danto seemed so different from my culturally threadbare, idea-shallow background. And Danto's ocular disability seemed so apt and romantic. His was a turning inward, an opening up, rather than the closing down and limitation that deafness represented to me in those days.

I received fat envelopes from Columbia, Oberlin, and Harpur, and an emaciated one from Princeton. This was a better response than my high school applications had elicited, but I still felt stung by the Princeton rejection—my Bronx Science dishonor all over again. While I clearly did not belong to the upper echelons, Columbia's urban and even Jewish flavor permitted me to slide in the back door. Financially it also made the most sense. Between my parents' unions (my father belonged to the International Ladies' Garment Workers Union and my mother, who worked as an alterations hand at a department store, to the Retail Clerks International), the New York State Regents' Scholarship, and the monies provided by Columbia, I had a full scholarship, including room, and a work-study job that would pay for my board.

I was jubilant. I would be joining an intellectual community and leaving home. I could hardly breathe on that September day when I rode the subway to my new earthly paradise. At the orientation meeting there were two lines, one for commuters and one for residents. I quickly joined the line of boys waiting to be assigned their rooms. As I glanced around, I felt the oddity of this moment. Surrounded by mainly prep schoolers in a wood-paneled hall on a venerable campus, I was suddenly intimidated. As I reached the window labeled "Residents," I spoke my name. The woman behind the metal bars shuffled through cards and then barked, "Wrong line! You're a commuter. Over there!" She pointed perfunctorily to the left, where boys who looked more like me were standing—kids from the Bronx, from Harlem and Bedford Stuyvesant.

I shuffled over in a kind of dream state. I was a commuter? I would continue to live in the one-bedroom apartment with my father sucking on the filaments of pot roast caught in his teeth? With my mother bringing out the dessert of tinned fruit cocktail? Was I caught in some cosmic mistake? I numbly waited in the commuter line, got my papers taken care of, and returned home.

When I broke the horrendous news to my mother, she was overjoyed. I wouldn't be leaving her just before my seventeenth birthday. I would stay home, as my brother had done.

My depression was immeasurable. I could have gone to Oberlin or Harpur College, but because I was lured by the aura of the Ivy League, seduced into a life that was clearly not mine, I would paradoxically end up living at home. I would trek down each day on the infernal IRT while my prep school brothers rose freshly from their crisp sheets and appeared in class in a matter of convenient and privileged minutes.

My mother tried to console me. She would make new bedspreads. I could choose a new color for the wall-to-wall carpet, changing from the royal blue carpet and orange bedspreads to the tweedier and more tasteful combination of browns I had wanted. I could try to make my room look like a suite at Oxford or Cambridge.

I looked at the bedroom I shared with my father. I had tried to personalize it: the few books I had read in high school were ensconced in a Danish modern bedroom unit, and a poster of Portugal (I had gotten it from a travel agent) showed white-washed walls and burros on a sun-baked street. A small reproduction depicted an elongated Modigliani mother with almond eyes and long hair nursing her elongated, almond-eyed baby. (I had picked it up gratis from an exhibition at IBM's gallery.) Here I was supposed to return each evening, rather like a male version of Cinderella. D. H. Lawrence by day, Abey the Fishman by night. I was close to a nervous breakdown.

I spent the next few days in a dorm on campus during freshman orientation. My old high school chums Marty Finklestein, Charley Goldstein, and Eugene Barrios had also been admitted with me to Columbia, and we kept the De Witt Clinton fires burning. My orientation roommate was named Stephen Demby, also a Jewish kid from New York, but from Bronx High School of Science. We all had to wear sky-blue beanies (class number '70 in white appeared on the front), name tags, and sports jackets with ties as we went on our appointed rounds. My father saved my beanie and wore it for at least a year when he turned seventy, seeing the number on the hat as a celebration of his age.

After about a week of classes, I received a phone call saying that a senior who had gone to China had failed to return. I could have his single room. I was freed from my exile! I could live on campus! And in my own room, for the first time in my life! Other first-year students had to share rooms or suites, while I had the luxury of a private one.

I was no longer an outsider. Or so I thought.

When I entered my simple room, equipped with the essentials—a bed, a desk, a bureau, and a sink—I felt gloriously independent. I was now a resident of New York City, not a kid in my deaf parents' apartment. I decorated the room immediately. In a garbage can in Chinatown I found a etching of a gentlewoman, nicely framed in oak. In a used furniture store I purchased a group photo of students at St. Paul's School in 1889. I aimed for tweeds and Victorian comfort, for some notion of a writerly, intellectual existence far from my parent's Danish modern, wall-to-wall kitsch. Since it was 1966, elements of the counterculture filtered into my decor as the semester went on. I added a Day-Glo Peter Max poster. A large photo of Sigmund Freud peered at me when I rolled down my shade. My mother made a slipcover with matching bolsters so I could pretend my bed was a couch. I took up pipe-smoking and bought Balkan Sobranie tobacco (which smelled like camel dung, probably because it was made with it). I used sepia ink to pen letters on Eaton's Highland Rag stationery with its frayed edges and rough surfaces. Howie and I decided to conduct a "correspondence," which we modeled on what we imagined two English gentleman would scribble to each other in their spare hours.

I really didn't have spare hours. Stretching myself through the discourses of Plato and Aristotle, training a rat I called Nestor in a Skinner box, trying to read Hegel and Descartes, figuring out the structure of the Gothic cathedral, and plowing through Browning's poetry filled my agenda. It was a heady experience after the provincial training I had received in high school. Far away seemed the couch on which my father snored with his copy of the *Daily News* on his lap, and even farther the kitchen where my mother chopped liver. The Deaf Club, sign language—all seemed remote. I tried to keep it that way.

My first grades arrived. I had done poorly. My paper about youth and age in the Greek world came back heavily annotated in red pen. I suspected that the other kids who had gone to prep school must be doing much better than I was. They had read some of this material before, and they knew how to write in a way I did not. I was puzzled and distraught. Had it turned out that the Princeton Alumnus was correct? That I really was not made of the right stuff?

Howie had enrolled at City College and was living at home. I was furious with his father for having made the decision to buy a car rather than spend the extra money it might take to send his son to a college like mine. Howie came to visit, staying in my dorm room a few times, but he decided I had become "stuck up"—the word universally used by Bronx kids to describe anyone who changed accents or aspired to leave the neighborhood. Howie commented on how I had begun to wear wide-wale corduroy and hip-hugger bell-bottoms, leaving the workshirted, chino-sporting crew behind. We began to drift apart, although a few years hence we would share an apartment on Broadway.

I slogged through the famous Humanities and Contemporary Civilization courses. My education was based on obscuring my virtual absence of prior training. Each grammatical mistake, each solecism, was a lash on my intellectual skin, branding me "poor," "child of the deaf," "uncouth." When my composition teacher, Richard Fadem, handed back my paper on "Lear's Turn toward Madness," he circled in red a sentence in which I described Lear as "raging and commanding the fundament." His marginal notation, "Look this one up," seared me—especially after I did look it up.

The Contemporary Civilization course made me question my religious beliefs. I had grown up orthodox, and while I had stopped going to synagogue, I kept kosher. (My brother no longer did.) As I began to read about other religions, I came to see that Judaism was only one form of consciousness. I could not imagine that only Jews would be saved, any more than I could believe that only Christians would be. So I abandoned my religious beliefs, although it was more difficult for me to abandon being kosher. It took the unobjectionable blandness of the chicken salad sandwiches at Chock Full O' Nuts to accomplish that.

As a typical product of the American public school system, I had never learned about Marxism. Even though my parents were workers, the only proletarian sense I got from my father and mother was some pride in trade unionism. In his youth, my father's connections with his trade unions had given him some leftist consciousness, but as the unions grew conservative, so did he. Without a radical analysis, I had no way of explaining how it was that my own education was inferior to that of my blazer-wearing peers. I could only claim "street smarts" as my legacy and advantage. I had no understanding of why other people had different lives, went on vacation to places other than the Borscht Belt hotels and Jewish Philanthropies' summer camps. In my Contemporary Civilization class I actually read a little of Marx, Fourier, Engels and began to understand how such disparities occurred.

Every Friday I left this new world of ideas and returned to my parents' apartment for Shabbos dinner. I walked down the long, sterile hallway of the apartment building, entered the glorified two rooms, sat in front of the mural of Venice, and ate my mother's chicken. There was an unreal sense of returning to the gloom, the limited expanse. I can't remember ever telling my parents what I was learning. Then I would take the subway back to Columbia, clutching my mother's meager food, which I kept cool on the window ledge so I might eat it for a day or two.

My life proceeded in usual fashion until one day in the spring of 1968, when a group of students decided to demonstrate in Morningside Park. I had always cast a jaded eye on Students for a Democratic Society (SDS). They all seemed to be kids from the suburbs, from wealthier families; I see now that their enthusiasm and conviction came from a sense of entitlement that I never possessed. When they talked blithely about forming a worker-student alliance, I thought of how my father and his cronies would have laughed at the idea.

The strike began innocuously enough. Columbia had intended to build a new gymnasium, and the site chosen was Morningside Park. With racial tensions high following Martin Luther King's assassination, and with Harlem just to the east, student groups thought Columbia was exercising a *droit de seigneur* over public lands. An arrest led to further protests, and then we stormed the academic buildings and occupied them.

Those were exciting, heady days. We met, voted, set up communal living arrangements, barricaded doors and windows, and even took as hostage for a few days the dean of Columbia College. We were suddenly in the news, on the radio and television. I found myself in Hamilton Hall, home of the English department. Instead of being an isolated student facing professors in the corridors, I was now camping out in their offices, sitting in their chairs, and listening to Dylan and the Stones late at night. I remember having a brief fling with another student, making out under some professor's towering file cabinet.

Clashes between right-wing and left-wing students became common, with the conservative athletes having the physical advantage. I was shocked to see Irwin Glickes, who had interviewed me two years earlier, leading a pack of angry football players against one of the buildings and inciting them to break in.

From the beginning I was not ambivalent. I was enough of an outsider to know what oppression looks like. I was never a leader of the strike, never a member of SDS, but I was as active as anyone. Living for almost a month in the buildings, I became part of something I had sought all my life: a community of people actively applying their intellectual and philosophical opinions to a political reality. My parents' learned helplessness was something I could leave behind without abandoning the issues their oppression represented.

I did not tell my parents much about what I was doing. My father and mother read about it in the *Daily News* and begged me not to get involved. "You poor," they correctly pointed out. "You lose scholarship, no college. Be nice, respectful, good." But this was my moment in history, and I didn't care about personal consequences.

The campus turned into an agora. Once I saw Sigmund Diamond, editor of the *Political Science Quarterly,* for whom I worked, haranguing some students at night. Drawn like a moth to this fire, I argued with him. Later I was fired from my job.

The Grateful Dead performed an impromptu concert in front of the student center. We held hands, sang, and danced. I thought of my own life and what a long strange trip it had been, from East Tremont Avenue in the Bronx to this hallowed, ivy campus. My picture was in the Sunday *New York Times Magazine* and in *Harper's.* My generation had changed something, perhaps forever.

On the evening of the "bust," as it was called, I went out for a walk. It was a warm spring night. Hundreds of police officers were streaming onto the campus. I ran back to Fayerweather Hall, to which I had moved after African American students had taken Hamilton Hall for their own, to alert my comrades. We broke up into three groups: those who would resist violently, those who would resist nonviolently, and those who would walk out. I opted for the last group.

Then the carnage began. The police axed their way through the doors. I heard screaming, crying, and saw blood. (Ironically, the students and faculty who were hurt the worst were the ones who had refrained from taking sides until the last minute. The famous poster of a bloodied student holding up his fingers in a "V" of peace portrayed just such a fence-sitter who had finally taken a stand.) This was the largest arrest in United States history. Over five hundred of us went down to the police stations. In the buses a bizarre sense of calm prevailed, and one wag even pulled the cord to indicate that the driver should stop at the next bus stop. We all laughed.

From the precinct we were put in paddy wagons and taken to the Tombs. I had only heard about this infamous jail on television. As I held onto the bars of the cell, the romance of the moment began to wear thin. I couldn't get out simply by willing, asking, arguing, quoting lines from Shakespeare. This was jail.

After a while a woman from Legal Aid arrived. She asked us who could post bail. The only one who came to mind was my Republican, conservative brother. I was sure he would find the phone call surprising. To his credit, he vouched for me, and years later he told me that he admired me for taking a principled stand.

Our court-appointed lawyers seemed compassionate and arranged for our hearings a month later. We were charged with criminal trespass; we pleaded innocent; the judge struck the gavel. Then suddenly I was on the street, alone and dazed. On the subway trip uptown, I wondered if it would matter to the other haggard riders that I had just spent the night in jail.

After the bust, the campus had become an occupied zone. The police, strictly kept off campus before the strike, were now an occupying force. I remember seeing my professor Fred Dupee with a black eye from the night before; he had tried to prevent the police from entering the buildings.

I was beginning to feel ill. In fact, I had mononucleosis but did not know it yet. I went to see my parents. I had been dreading this visit, since they now knew of my arrest. I walked down the cheerless corridor and saw my father standing at the door. He raised his forefinger and started to open his mouth. My mother grabbed him and signed, "Let him eat supper first!" We sat in silence as I ate the pot roast, my father waiting to harangue me. No sooner was the last bite swallowed than he began. "Stupid! Now all lost! You lose scholarship. They kick you out! Why? What reason?"

I tried to explain my motivations, but of course it was useless. How could I possibly explain to them the idea of the justice that I felt I was upholding? They had suffered under various yokes, bearing their burden, not protesting affronts, humiliations, low-paying jobs, discrimination. That was how they survived. Now I had violated their ways. My father was furious; my mother, hurt. My father had written a groveling letter to the dean—the very dean I had held hostage—begging him to spare my academic life. The dean, who had no fewer than five hundred students in the same boat, wrote back a fair and measured letter reassuring my father that many good students had been in the strike and that things would work out.

I left home feeling very isolated. My fever was rising. I packed my backpack for a planned trip to Europe. (I had saved my earnings from a previous summer job as a bellhop at the Concord Hotel.) My lawyer had deferred my court hearing until September, when charges against all of us would eventually be dropped. I went to the airport, shouldering the burden of my parents' condemnation along with my gear. I was going to stay in London with my Aunt Betty for a few days, meet up with Howie, and then hitchhike for three months around England and Europe. As I boarded the charter flight along with many other students who had just been in the strike, it felt as if I was winging my way into possibility. I was eighteen years old. I had never been on an airplane before. I had my old life behind me and new one ahead.

The trip would take eighteen hours, stopping in Gander, Reykjavik, Shannon, and then London. To compensate us for the inconvenience, Pam Am offered free drinks for the whole flight. As I drank wine and stared off at the skies, I felt myself leaving everything. My parents' world seemed to grow smaller and less visible. I ran through everything I knew from the time when I had almost drowned in Crotona Park: my school years, summer camp, the world of the Deaf. Alongside these played the fugue of new thoughts: of Goethe, Homer, Marx, my girlfriends, the strike.

On the intercom the pilot told us to look out the window. For the first time I saw the Northern Lights, shimmering cobalt, emerald, and orange. So many things I had never seen. Tomorrow seemed to fill with color as I imagined all that lay ahead beyond the blackness, beyond my sense of silence.

Epilogue

Decades have passed since that flight to Europe. I am now a professor of literature and cultural studies at Binghamton University, a part of the State University of New York. Bella Mirabella is my wife of twenty years (and friend of longer). Our son, Carlo, is now nineteen, about the age I had reached when I boarded that plane. Our daughter, Francesca, is sixteen.

How many of my life's achievements have resulted from my having working-class Deaf parents, and how much has been accomplished despite that circumstance? Hard to say. I have written a number of books and articles, and I have achieved that limited kind of fame whereby certain people in academe know my name and my work. Having to serve as interpreter for my parents gave me complex language skills, as well as confidence in my own know-how. Furthermore, I recognize that my will to persevere despite difficult odds came to me from my father, whose competitive spirit was inculcated in me at an early age. My mother, in contrast, taught me not to expect too much and not to become overly upset about failure. I developed a sense about injustice and the need to fight for fairness and equality because of my daily encounters with the demeaning or dismissive ways the hearing world treated my parents. I can now say that my experience of growing up in a Deaf family is one that I would never surrender or exchange, even though as a child I yearned for a "normal" family.

From birth I entered my parents' world of silence and sign language. Still, I knew deafness only instinctively, without reflection or understanding. Like the fish, I could never be the one to discover water. My parents, born at the beginning of the twentieth century in England, were brought up in an unenlightened world where the deaf were viewed as inferior, pitiable people, deprived of language and therefore of reason, a bit better off than the blind in their mobility and somewhat akin to the mentally retarded in their thoughts and communication. Although my parents knew better than that, they often had little choice but to assume the role of inferiors. I too saw their deafness as a profound problem, one that I could overcome only by flight from their world.

My parents asserted that their deafness was an insignificant feature of their life. As my father said over and over again, "We are the same as everyone else, just deaf. That's all." Our relatives and friends agreed. People would always say to me, "It's amazing how your parents could raise two clever boys like you and your brother." When people asked me what it was like to grow up in a deaf family, I always said it was pretty much the same as being in any other family, only my parents could not hear. I described the minor inconveniences of having to pound on the floor with my foot to call my parents, rather than just saying "Mom" or "Dad" as other children did, or of having to be the one who made phone calls. My parents felt that their deafness did not impede their functioning in their world; likewise, our hearing relatives wanted to normalize my parents and their lives. As a child, therefore, I felt that my parents were right: their deafness did not diminish them at all.

At the same time, I carried a deep embarrassment and humiliation for being born of deaf parents. I wished they could be normal, like those of my friends. I wanted parents who could call other parents on the telephone. I wanted a dad who could saunter down the street and say "Hi!" to the neighbors, instead of producing a guttural howl. When I was in public, I burned with resentment and shame as hearing people gaped at my parents talking to each other in sign language. Once, when the much older brother of my friend said that my father talked "like an Indian," I leapt on him, like a flea trying to attack an elephant. When my mother came to school on visiting day, as I described, I did not know how to handle her benign presence, watching everything but hearing nothing.

Disabilities today are more respected by people and protected by the law. But the term "disability," with its synthesis of understanding, awareness, and fairness, did not exist in my childhood. Further, the idea that the Deaf were not disabled but were a linguistic minority had not been thought of even remotely. Instead, I had two "deaf and dumb" parents—or, worse, "dummies." Even people who did not gape at them still condescended. No *Children of a Lesser God* made their world understandable and legitimate to hearing people. No Marlee Matlin presented an attractive image to the deaf person. Oliver Sacks had not yet written *Seeing Voices*. Gallaudet University was Gallaudet College in those days; it had no Deaf studies department and was administered by hearing people. No telecommunication devices permitted easy contact between the outside world and my parents: no captioned television, no hearing assistance devices in the theater. The world knew only the exceptional case of Helen Keller, who justified her "handicaps" by writing books that a hearing world could understand.

I saw the intelligent and lively side of my parents and their friends at the Deaf Club. I knew that my father and mother were capable of subtle communication, and that sign language was as adequate, capacious, and poetic as any other language. I could tell my parents almost anything that any other kid in the Bronx could tell his or her parents. I knew my mother was loving and devoted, working hard at a low-paying job to earn the necessities of life. I knew my father was a gifted artist and capable writer. He wrote a column for the national deaf magazine and authored plays that he and his friends performed at the Deaf Club. I also knew, when I looked at the pile of old *New York Times* issues in the closet, that headlines were blazoned with my father's name for having been a world-class race-walker, all the while working as a sewing-machine operator in a sweatshop.

I knew all this, and I defended my parents from the unheard slings and arrows of the hearing world. Yet it was my aim and my parents' desire that I be accepted by that world, forsaking my deaf and working-class origins and starting my own upwardly mobile life. I should meld with the intellectual world and forget my origins. Once I was in graduate school, Steven Marcus (who knew my background, and who himself had grown up in the Bronx) suggested that I write a dissertation on gesture in literature, since I had knowledge of sign language and therefore of the nuances of nonverbal meanings. I quickly dismissed the idea, pointing out correctly that sign language is a true language and not really gesture per se. But my real reason was that I did not want to build my career as a scholar on the very subject to which I was fashioning my life in opposition.

My mother died when I was in graduate school, and my father about ten years later. I taught literature at distinguished colleges and universities. My connection with deafness began to seem distant, like a hazy recollection of a life-threatening automobile accident. When I would tell colleagues or friends about my upbringing, they would always be amazed. At this point I was not embarrassed; rather, I shared their amazement that I had gone so far from where I had begun. (Of course, I would have to answer the inevitable questions: "But how did you learn to speak?" "Say something to me in sign language.")

I met Bella Mirabella when I was twenty-five and we were both teaching at Queens College. In the ensuing years several key events awakened me to the fact that I had never really left deafness behind.

One seemed a minor incident at the time, though I have since remembered it frequently. Bella and I were visiting a friend at her house on Martha's Vineyard. Our friend's neighbor was a psychoanalyst who invited us over for cocktails. In the course of the conversation, she discovered that my parents were deaf and became interested in my early life. At one point she said, "Well, you must be very depressed, considering your childhood." Bella and I laughed at this observation, both for its conversational left-feet and because no one was more of a cutup, bon vivant, and generally humorous person than I. Yet the observation nettled me. Bella and I would often refer to those words and joke about them, but perhaps I felt the subtle graze of truth. Why would my childhood link me with depression?

A second inkling that my connection to deafness was more profound than I had realized came shortly after the first. Because Bella and I were thinking about having a child, we went for genetic counseling. (She carried a trait for Mediterranean anemia.) I did not consider deafness an issue. When we talked to the genetic counselor, I answered a routine question about my parents.

"Oh, were they born deaf?" she asked with inquiring eyes.

"No," I answered, as I had done my entire life. "My mother contracted spinal meningitis at the age of seven, and my father became deaf at one or two after being dropped down the stairs by his aunt."

"What was the exact diagnosis of his deafness?"

"Well, to tell you the truth, I don't really know."

"The only reason I ask is because early childhood deafness is often difficult to diagnose until tests can be administered."

I was unsettled. It never occurred to me that my father could have been born deaf. He was dropped down the stairs, got an infection, and his eardrums had to be cut out, since he was born in 1898 and there were no antibiotics. He would always point under his ear to a small scar.

But now that I thought about it, his explanation made little sense. He said his aunt had dropped him down the stairs. Later, an uncle who was playing the violin stopped suddenly and exclaimed in Yiddish,

"Morris can't hear!" But then what were the scars doing under his ears? Wouldn't his parents have known that he could not hear if his eardrums had already been removed? So why did his uncle remark in surprise? I had to look into this further. Perhaps I was closer to deafness than I thought. Could it be that deafness was lurking in my genes, waiting to burst forth into the ears of the unborn? Would I be signing to my children as I did to my parents?

My father was still alive at that time. I went to visit him in the one-bedroom apartment in Upper Manhattan where I had spent my teen years. Everything was the same—the wallpaper mural of Venice in the dining alcove, the plastic covers on the couch, the *Daily News* open on the Formica table. My father was looking older at eighty-one, with cancer slowly marching from his prostate to his bones. But he greeted me warmly and signed to me, telling all the details of his day. He was always a great storyteller, reveling in each ordinary particular. Sniffing, throat clearing, and assorted mouth noises accompanied his signs and guttural words. I usually listened as patiently as I could to his tales of going to the post office to mail a special letter or of walking down Broadway to the Deaf Club, but on this day I interrupted him.

"I have to ask you a question. How did you become deaf?"

He began telling me the story about the aunt, the stairs, the scar. Then I realized with a shock: *there was only one scar.* Only one eardrum could have been removed. *Then why was he deaf in both ears?*

I quizzed him on all the details. Only then did I realize that, although he was telling his own story, he was merely the repository of a confused set of narratives. Obviously no one knew what had happened. If there had been medical intervention, the details were probably not conveyed to his immigrant, half-fluent parents. And in 1899 the British doctors might even have had little idea of what they were doing. If childhood deafness is difficult to detect now, how difficult must it have been then? My father might well have been born deaf, and his uncle might have been the first to realize it.

I started to become terribly concerned. I had to acknowledge that I had not left deafness behind as neatly as I had thought. When Carlo was born, I spent a lot of time shaking keys over his head and calling to him. I did the same with Francesca. But everything was in order: the children could hear. With that knowledge the circle seemed to close. I was now patriarch of my own nuclear family, whose physical normalcy replaced the stigma surrounding my deaf family.

When I received the call that my father had died, I rushed over to the nursing home and looked with pain upon his stilled body. No longer would he sign. The day before he had been in a kind of coma. I shook him and he opened his eyes. I signed, "How are you?" "Fine, thank you," he replied weakly, his fingers forming the words. Then his eyes rolled back in his head.

He had been in the hospital for six months, his wasted corpse a mute testimony to the ravages of cancer. His head was twisted slightly as if looking over his right shoulder, and his expressive eyes were lifeless and filmed over. I closed them and sat for some time with him, feeling the sadness and puzzlement that come from seeing the definitive end of a parent whose life had so filled mine. My fingers held no more words. Both of my parents were now dead. As I walked home, the sun rose in a glorious dawn over Morningside Park. I felt a weight lift as my father's long illness, and vastly longer deafness, came to an end.

Many deaf friends came to my father's funeral, and I had an opportunity to see all the wonderful, warm, and lively people who had colored my childhood so vividly. I knew that I would not be seeing much of them in the future. A few months later I took my son to the Hanukkah party at the Deaf Club, as my father and mother had taken me, but it was clearly a connection I was losing.

My brother and I did not continue speaking sign language with each other, since we had normally used it only to speak with our parents. I taught my children some simple words and phrases, but only out of nostalgia.

When I was thirty-three I entered psychotherapy. The issues of my childhood came up rather quickly, and I began reluctantly to explore my feelings toward my parents' deafness. Despite my therapist's repeated queries about how I felt, I could never generate much anger toward my parents. They had done the best they could, I would explain, and yes, I had had some minor inconveniences in my life. Although I could say that I might have been angry at my mother or my father for some aspect of their deafness—their inability to hear my cries at night, my having to take care of them rather than their taking care of me, my mother's passivity, my father's irrationality, their simplistic view of morality and of the world—I could never really feel anger.

When I thought about parenting my own children, I could see how important hearing was. When my son or daughter called out at night, I would arise and comfort him or her in a way that no one had comforted me or my brother. We had had to do all the comforting ourselves, as we lay in bed terrified, or wet, or hungry, or tangled up in the bedclothes. We seemed to have become good at coping, at getting along without help. But now I was discovering that I needed help after all, and that I had suppressed a lot of emotions in order to survive and get along in the world.

I remember watching a television film called *Love Is Never Silent,* produced by the deaf actress Julianna Fjeld. As I sat alone that night, the kids asleep and my wife at a meeting, I viewed with fascination the compelling story of a young hearing girl with deaf parents. I wept profusely and wrote in my journal, "I am afraid that if I really open this up I will never stop crying." Though my parents were dead, and though I was hearing, deafness was in me. I had not run away at all; I had only gone around the block.

❖

One day my writer friend Eva Hoffman, who was working as an editor at the *New York Times,* suggested that I review *Lessons in Laughter* by Bernard Bragg, an actor who had helped found the National Theater for the Deaf. After my piece appeared, I received a letter telling me of an organization called CODA (Children of Deaf Adults). The writer, Randy Meyers, was the son of my father's close friend "Red" Meyers. He invited me to attend the annual CODA conference. I called Randy, for whom I had babysat when I was in my teens and he in his crib. By now he was coordinator of mental health services for the deaf in Illinois. He had done what I could never have imagined doing: he had stayed with deafness.

My wife had long suggested that I try to write about my childhood. I had already contributed a piece to *Parents* magazine on how hearing my daughter play the violin had led me to reflect on how my own parents could never hear me play my recorder. I was also working on a somewhat autobiographical screenplay about a boy with deaf parents coming of age in the 1960s in the Bronx. So I thought I might write an article about this strange convention, or at least generate some ideas for my book or for the screenplay.

When I arrived at the Texas School for the Deaf, a group of people wearing cowboy hats and bandannas burst into a round of welcoming applause, accompanied by hoots and hollers. People foisted on me my own hat and scarf, insisting that I wear this ridiculous outfit immediately. My doubts about coming to the conference escalated. How could I, who had spent my life avoiding humiliation, allow a ten-gallon hat to slide down over my ears?

At a special meeting for newcomers, I saw hearing people signing with each other. I could not understand why hearing people would do this.

An attractive blonde woman about my age stood and introduced herself as Millie Brother, CODA's founder. As she began to describe how she had felt a need to form such a group, I started to relax a bit. She was intelligent, articulate, and . . . well, like me. Several other panelists described how they had felt as newcomers, how odd and strange it all was, and how moving. People related how they had cried, and tissue boxes began circulating as other members of the audience sympathized. I found this all rather difficult and began planning to change my airline ticket for an earlier departure.

After dinner in the combination gymnasium, lunch room, and auditorium, an ice-breaker session involved party games and tricks. We had to pass balloons to our partners without touching them with our hands, and so on. Rather than breaking the ice, for me these activities created glacial chill. What was I doing here among these cowboy-hatted idiots? Spirited shrieks and guttural emanations filled the air.

Then we adjourned to a hospitality suite. I grabbed a beer. It seemed as if most attendees were overweight women in their forties and fifties. The majority were interpreters for the deaf, or people who still worked with the deaf. I thought to myself that people who had accomplished anything outside the world of the deaf had obviously not come here. But I did meet a fellow whose father had been good friends with mine; I instantly felt a bond with him. I also encountered an old childhood friend, now a psychotherapist.

Some people wanted to go out to a nightclub, but I opted for bed. In my room, with the lights out, I experienced the feeling of solitariness. I had felt alone in my family, the hearing outsider. I had felt alone in the community, the son of the deaf people. Now I felt alone here, someone who was a child of deaf adults but who did not identify with the deaf. In that dark, lonely place I felt the brush of isolation and mortality. I was cut off from everything again.

Several years later, I relived this newcomer experience at second hand when Gerald accompanied me to his first CODA conference. I had asked him to attend before, but he had always held back. Finally, perhaps because of our mutual involvement with publication of our parents' love letters, he agreed.

On a hot July morning in 1998 we set off down the New Jersey Turnpike, embarking on what would be our most extended period together since childhood. Now I was almost fifty and he almost sixty. We reminisced, and Gerald talked a bit about his feelings. He said, as we sailed past the industrial wasteland of Elizabeth, New Jersey, that there would be no difference between when he was dead and the life he was living now. As I had in the past, I advised therapy; again he refused. But his very willingness to make this journey was a sign that he was not as dead as he claimed.

When we arrived at the conference site, I rushed him off to the newcomers' orientation. He emerged an hour or two later, looking a bit stunned, and said he was going to have some lunch. Although he clearly wanted "down time," I grabbed him and directed him to a breakout session. After a few hours he reappeared, looking wide-eyed and reporting that things had gotten very emotional. It was clear that while he found this interesting, he also found it uncomfortable. Though this conference in Alexandria, Virginia, lacked the ten-gallon hats that had been de rigueur at my first CODA conference in Texas, I could sense that Gerald also viewed the attendees as quite unlike himself.

During supper and the socializing he stayed near me. Seeing many of these hearing people signing and talking like deaf people was a bit shocking to him. (While the attendees speak perfectly good English, many enjoy the intimacy and fellow feeling that comes from speaking in sign language. Some also imitate or try on their parents' voices.) That evening he visited the hospitality suite, a site of much storytelling and hilarity. For the first time I saw him relax and enjoy the experience. He loved the stories, and he laughed and cried at various tales.

That night, in our hotel room, we automatically chose the beds we had occupied as kids: mine on the right, his on the left. I had the strangest feeling of being back on Clinton Avenue in the Bronx. We said good night and talked a little in the dark.

The next morning Gerald awoke with an expression I had seen many times before. With a hard, tight look around his thin lips, he announced that he really did not want to attend any more of the conference. He preferred to take a vacation. He would visit the Holocaust Museum in Washington and then walk along the Potomac.

I was disappointed but not surprised, given that my own initial response to a CODA conference had involved contemplating an earlier flight home. I had sensed that I had made a mistake in encouraging him to attend.

"Fine," I said. "But just come to the siblings' session."

This was the session that I had been fantasizing about for years. Formerly estranged siblings sometimes burst into tears, overcoming years of emotional distance. Or smoldering rivalries occasionally blaze forth into fiery emotions. Either of these alternatives would have been fine with me.

Gerald agreed to attend.

We all sat in a circle, passing a baton, and the person who held the baton spoke. Many cried. When the baton reached Gerald, he took it, paused a second, and said, "Emotions were not encouraged in my family. This is difficult for me, but I'm happy to be here." He then passed the baton to me.

I was shocked, because most people had said more. Holding the baton, I spoke of many of the issues I have written about in this book, saying how I hoped my brother could open up by coming to CODA so we could be bound closer by friendship, not merely by blood. I cried. By the time the baton reached him again, I was hopefully expectant. He said a few words and again passed it to me.

At the end of the session we agreed we needed to talk. We returned to our room and for the first time in many years—perhaps ever—we spoke of the issues between us. We both cried. I felt that he finally understood my pain about our past. He told me of his hurt when I did not telephone him first with the news of my son's birth. He also described how I had wounded him by failing to attend some of his family's functions. I spoke of how difficult it was for me to get close to him when he was so emotionally remote. The differences in our needs and our boundaries for intimacy became clear. But what became equally clear was that we loved each other, had hurt each other, and were hoping to heal our old wounds by exposing and sharing our pain. At the end of our conversation we hugged each other.

True to his word, Gerald did not attend any other formal sessions. Instead, he found his connection to his Deaf past through talking with people, through the warm family feelings that others lavished on him, and most of all through the entertainment, comedy, song-signing, and storytelling. I watched him on the final night as one talented man told the poignant and funny story of his relation to his Deaf experience. With my own misty gaze I surveyed the room and saw many people, including Gerald, laughing through collective tears.

One of that evening's entertainments was a dramatic reading of our parents' love letters. I had corralled two actors, with an interpreter behind each, to read the letters much in the manner of the Broadway play *Love Letters*. I stood beside the stage and watched this amazing moment in which my obscure, working-class parents' experience became the object of rapt attention on the part of a 350-member audience. When the reading concluded, the applause was enthusiastic. I joined the actors on stage. The audience called for my brother. From the back of the room, Gerald wended his way forward as they cheered for him, for us, for our parents. He mounted the stage and, for the first time in his life, felt the admiration and warm welcome of a community. He beamed with tearful eyes.

So much distance covered, so many years passed, from our one-bedroom apartment, from loneliness and terror, to this moment of acceptance and love. Now, for both of us, it was worth the trip.

We would never have experienced that performance, or shared that feeling of communion with each other, had I not overcome the feelings of isolation that had swept over me during that night in my single room at the Texas CODA conference years earlier. When I awoke the next morning, I resolved to return to the sessions.

I heard one participant describe his personal journey through deafness. He spoke of his love toward his parents, but also of his anger. He described how his mother never knocked on his bedroom door, because she could not have heard his reply; instead, she simply barged in. He mourned this absence of privacy. I then realized for the first time that doors were never closed in our apartment. He told of hiding a letter from his school that invited his folks to Parents' Day. He painfully remembered being a young child who had to relay the doctor's message that his mother needed a hysterectomy. This moving, intelligent account made me feel a connection at last.

Attending other sessions in which people shared their personal stories, I experienced a powerful conjunction between my childhood sign-language life and my adult intellectual life. I suddenly felt certain that I could recover the child, deaf-self that I had left behind, merging it with my hearing self.

After one particularly emotional session, I walked outside and saw a swing set for the schoolchildren. A woman had also drifted out from the group. Together, wordlessly and instinctively, we were drawn toward the swings, lured by their suggestion of a childhood happiness that had been so illusory for us.

We sat in adjacent swings and began to pump. The swing carried me toward the sky, now suddenly bluer, and the sweat on my body and the tears on my face evaporated in the exhilarating breeze. I put my head back and sailed up with a glee that I probably never experienced as a child. The woman next to me was similarly absorbed. Strangers, yet not, we seized the sadness, the grief and anger, and cast it into the sky.

Creative Nonfiction

Typeset in 9/14 Stone Serif
with Helvetica Neue Extended
and Avalon display
Designed by Paula Newcomb
Composed by Jim Proefrock
at the University of Illinois Press
Manufactured by Thomson-Shore, Inc.

University of Illinois Press
1325 South Oak Street
Champaign, IL 61820-6903
www.press.uillinois.edu